Just in Time
STRESS MANAGEMENT

Just in Time
STRESS MANAGEMENT

Brian Clegg

KOGAN
PAGE

Publisher's Note

Every possible effort has been made to ensure that the information contained in this book is accurate at the time of going to press, and the publishers and authors cannot accept responsibility for any errors or omissions, however caused. No responsibility for loss or damage occasioned to any person acting, or refraining from action, as a result of the material in this publication can be accepted by the editor, the publisher or any of the authors.

Previously published as Instant Stress Management

First South Asian Edition 2005
Reprinted 2008

Kogan Page India Private Limited
4737/23 Ansari Road,
Daryaganj
New Delhi 110 002

ISBN-10: 81-7554-122-9
ISBN-13: 978-81-7554-122-1

Published by Vinod Vasishtha for Kogan Page India Private Limited,
4737/23 Ansari Road, Daryaganj, New Delhi - 110 002.

Printed and bound at Raj Press, R-3, Inderpuri, New Delhi - 110 012

Contents

4 Exercises 1 – Assessing 19

5 Exercises 2 – Destressing 31

1

STRESS – WHAT'S ALL THE FUSS ABOUT?

INSTANT STRESS MANAGEMENT

Stress is a recognized killer and a major contributor to workplace illness. Companies are worried about stress because of reduced effectiveness; individuals can find that the impact of stress blights their health and happiness. Yet stress is a complex phenomenon. It can't be painted in black and white. We all need a degree of stress to drive us on to achieve. Neither total lack of stress nor stress to excess is good for you.

The ideal is to be able to understand your response to stress and to have an armoury of stress removal techniques and stress defences to employ when the going gets tough. The 'Instant' format is ideal for this topic – suffering from stress usually means that there is pressure on time. The ability to take a gradual approach to stress management that helps to modify your attitude to life without becoming an irritating chore is very appealing. Stress management also suffers from being associated in some quarters with alternative lifestyles and airy-fairy concepts, so by putting stress management in a down-to-earth series like the Instants, I hope to show that it can be a straightforward, business-like proposition.

Like the other books in the series, *Instant Stress Management* is built around more than 70 exercises, mostly taking five to 20 minutes, which can be used to control stress. There is also a shorter section of exercises to help to assess how stressed you are and where that stress is coming from. Each exercise has a star rating showing particular usefulness as physical control, emotional and spiritual control, and defence, plus a fun rating.

WHAT STRESS IS

The trouble with stress is that it's not a matter of right or wrong. We have been conditioned to see stress as purely negative because of handy slogans like 'stress kills'. But you can't live a slogan – and in this case you wouldn't want to. Stress is the impact of a demand on a human being. The source can be external or internal. The demand can be positive or negative. Arguably there is no life at all without stress.

At the physical level we have a pretty good understanding of what stress is about. When the brain senses a demand for exertion it signals the release of various hormones from glands around the body. These active agents, like adrenalin, noradrenalin and cortisol, prepare the body for action. Muscles tense up, the heart beats faster and the blood supply is concentrated where it is needed, moving away from 'low need' areas like the digestion and the skin. All this is designed to provide a wave of energy to enable you to react appropriately to the trigger: to fight or to run away. To survive.

THE BRAIN IN ACTION

Stress is always a balance of the physical and the mental. It helps in understanding stress to have a basic understanding of the brain's activity. The electrical activity of the brain has been typified by psychologists in four different categories. These are specified in the somewhat illiterate sequence of delta (0–3 activities per second), theta (3–7 activities per second), alpha (7–14 activities per second) and beta (14–28 activities per second).

In delta state the brain is hardly active at all. This is deep sleep, when the body seems to be undergoing physical repair activities. Theta is the state where rapid eye movement sleep takes place – the condition required for dreaming. This is thought to happen when the brain is reorganizing its information for more effective use. Alpha and beta are waking states. Alpha is unfocused – it's where you are daydreaming or letting your mind wander. Alpha is the creative state. Beta, on the other hand, is focused. It's the state you move into to get things done, to follow a plan.

The importance of all this for stress is that being in too high a mental state for a desired action is stressing. At the extreme, as your brain activity gets faster and faster, it can end up thrashing about, incapable of making decisions or solving problems. This is not helped by the fact that it is much easier to switch up a state than to switch down, hence the need for stress-relieving techniques to help us to switch down a state in a controlled way.

WE NEED STRESS

Stress has an important function. There are times when it is a genuine aid to survival – escaping a burning building or an attack. More often it is a driver to get the extra mile. You might be an athlete or an actor, a manager giving a business presentation or a firefighter. In any role, stress can make all the difference. Everyone who has ever gone on stage knows only too well that feeling in the pit of the stomach that says 'Why the hell am I here?' – but without that stress there wouldn't be the huge return that makes it all worthwhile.

Positive stress is the fuel that drives us beyond the commonplace. The very concept of being 'driven' implies a sort of stress. Without any stress, life would be reduced to the level of a grazing animal with everything supplied. No wants, no worries, no interests – not much of a life.

STRESS IN EXCESS

If things were that simple, stress management would be all about getting more stress, but there's a price to pay that means most of us suffer from too much stress rather than too little. There are two contributory factors. One is the added complexity and pace of life. Our bodies were designed for stress as a special case, but all too often it's the norm. The other problem is the nature of stressors. When we get the surge of adrenalin and other hormones, all too often we don't do anything to make use of those changes to our body. The requirement is not to fight or to run away – we just have to sit and take it. This happens with stresses as widely separated as the rigours of driving and bringing up children.

One-off examples of such stresses aren't as much of a problem, it's the combination of stress without a physical response and frequent, almost constant, exposure that does the real damage. Someone who is constantly on the edge of stress can be easily tipped into over-reaction – road rage is a classic example – by trivial incidents. And the body simply isn't built for long-term stress-heightened activity. Without an outlet, the outcome can be increased risk of heart disease and other medical conditions.

The impact of such harmful stress differs widely from individual to individual. Some of us have a more laid-back attitude to life; others will fly off the handle at the least provocation. As well as such internal inclination or disinclination to respond to stress, our position in life can have a significant effect. Research in the Civil Service has shown that there is a very strong correlation between stress levels and degrees of self-determination. Senior civil servants, who are very much in control of what they are doing from day to day, have a much lower rate of stress-related illness than cleaners and other staff whose workday is pre-programmed.

DOING SOMETHING ABOUT IT

It is reasonable to ask if there is anything we can actually do about the problems of stress, or whether, like death, we had better accept it because it's a certainty. There are limits to how much you can change your personality in order to reduce your bad reaction to stress. However, there is still a lot to be done. For example, the studies that have shown stress to be related to a level of self-determination explain the link in terms of attitude. If you have a positive attitude, helped by control, you are less liable to be badly stressed than if you have a negative attitude, always finding fault and never happy with the situation.

It's also necessary to bear in mind that the aim of stress management is not to eliminate stress totally. The good stress that gives you the edge when you need it is something you'll always want, it's the negative stress that has to be controlled. This can be approached in a number of ways. You can defend yourself from the stressors, stopping them from ever getting to you. You can counter the effects of stress physically, using exercise or drugs to counter the attack. Or you can resort to emotional and spiritual relief, bringing a calm to the inner self that results in less likelihood of developing a negative stress response.

This book can't provide all the answers. In some circumstances it will be necessary to get professional help, or to look to others to help to deal with your stress. But *Instant Stress Management* will give you a toolkit of anti-stress techniques to help in most circumstances.

2

STRESSORS

WHERE STRESS COMES FROM

When we're managing stress it helps to know where it's coming from. For any individual there are liable to be a range of causes, some very personal, some general to all of us. If you think through a typical day, you can see a set of classical stress inducers:

- A blaring noise from your alarm clock wakes you up.
- You are tired because you stayed up too late last night.
- You are worried about your promotion interview this afternoon.
- Your children demand your attention when you are in a hurry to get ready for work.
- You are late.
- Heavy traffic makes you later still.
- Bad drivers cut you up and slow you down.
- The computer isn't working properly again.
- When you ring support you get stuck in a voice-handling queue.

... and so on.

Stressors are attacking you from all sides – and from inside. The exercises in *Instant Stress Management* will provide you with tools to handle stress in yourself and others, and will look at some of the more common causes of stress. In general, the exercises emphasize the small, frequent causes of stress, as these are often the ones that we ignore at our peril. Everyone is aware of the stressful impact of a death in the family or of moving house. There is more need to flag up some of the lesser stressors that continuously nibble away at our sanity.

INTERNAL STRESSORS

It would be nice to blame 'them' for all our stress. If only they left me alone to get on with things, everything would be fine. Sadly, it's just not true. A sizeable chunk of bad stress comes from within. This can operate at a simple practical level. Your ability to take control of your time can have a significant impact on stress. Time management may seem a plodding, mechanical activity, but getting your time organized so that you have more room for the things you really want to do is an important contributor to stress management.

Equally important is the whole mix of emotional confusion that can erupt in any of us. Because our emotional sides are beyond conscious control, they can be a prime cause of stress. Your feelings can stress you long after you are out of reach of the original causes of stress. You might start with a small amount of external stress – your child is being very difficult, so you get angry and smack it. But the stress you then generate for yourself from guilt and frustration at your own lack of control can far outweigh the original trigger.

In our materialistic world, it might seem strange that a practical book should dwell on the spiritual, but spiritual influences cannot be ignored when it comes to internal stresses. Almost everyone feels the need for something more, something beyond the everyday; the lack of spiritual content in our lives can be a prime source of stress. This underlying need is reflected in the questions addressed by the major religions – 'What's the point?' 'Is there anything more to life?' 'You live and then you die and that's it?' Uncertainty about where life is taking us and the ever-present reality of death produce internal stress, while many find that spiritual sources provide a relief and defence against a whole range of stressors, not just the physical.

EXTERNAL STRESSORS

Although the internal is important, we can't ignore external stressors. They are there all the time. Some are immense one-off shocks to the system. Bereavement, moving house, divorce, going on holiday (yes, it causes stress). Others are small but constantly nagging – driving on congested roads or constant hassles at work. We have already seen that because, whatever the stress, our bodies react as if we are in physical danger, we end up with a potentially damaging hormonal reaction. This means that often there is more danger from the small but constantly present stresses than a big, one-off event. However, you do also need to be aware of the dangers when several big stressing events occur in one year. In Chapter 4 we will look at a number of ways of assessing your high-level and low-level stress states.

WHY ME?

Stress doesn't affect everyone in the same way. A number of reasons, mental and physiological, will determine how an individual responds to stress. Some of us are more quick-tempered or more naturally calm. Some of us have more self-esteem and feel more in control, hence are better able to let stress wash over us. Even our state of health will change our ability to cope with stress.

This doesn't mean that there's nothing to be done about it. We may not be able to (or even want to) change our personalities, but there is plenty that can be done to help even if you are naturally inclined to respond to stress in the wrong way, or to bring stress on yourself. That's the point of this book – to help with managing stress so that you can better your natural level of stress control.

MEDICAL STUFF

Care has to be taken when attempting stress management. Some apparent stress symptoms have a medical cause. If you are suffering from symptoms like dizziness, chest pains, palpitations and faintness, it's not enough to think that you are stressed and attempt to manage it – you could equally be suffering from a heart condition. If you have physical symptoms, make sure that you check with your GP rather than assuming that they are down to stress.

Similarly, inability to sleep or headaches or stomach conditions, all potentially stress-induced, can have physical causes that need treatment – don't make assumptions, check with the doctor. Finally, don't assume that depression is necessarily stress-induced. There are two clear forms of depression – exogenous, caused by external influences, and endogenous, coming from internal causes. An endogenous depression is totally unconnected to any stressors you may have and will not respond to stress management. Such a depression does not imply that you are mentally ill – it is a recognized physiological condition. Again, if you are suffering from depression or its consequences (sadness and misery, tiredness and sleep difficulties, eating disorders, difficulty concentrating or making decisions), check with your GP, don't make assumptions.

3

STRESS CONTROL

CONTROL AND RELIEF

So far the picture of stress has been fairly unpleasant. While we need an element of stress in our lives to add flavour and keep things moving, the level of stress we are all under far exceeds these requirements, and generally is of a destructive rather than constructive nature. We need mechanisms to bring stress under control and to relieve the damage it can cause. Broadly, we can divide ways of controlling our response to stress into three types – physical, emotional and spiritual. We can also build defences against stress, preventing the stress getting through in the first place.

PHYSICAL CONTROL

Stress is a physiological consequence of the stressor, and as such responds to physical control. At the extreme this can involve the use of drugs, but more frequently it can be a matter of giving the body the natural defences to be able to handle stress, and enabling a physical outlet when stress manifests itself.

Human beings have never before had such a sedentary life. Much work is now chair-bound, whether you are sitting in front of a computer screen or driving a car. The TV ensures that our entertainment is often low energy, too. We don't walk as much as we used to. Recent reports have shown that women, who traditionally had less of a problem with diseases caused by insufficient exercise, have now caught up with men. A major factor in being able to deal with stress is to be able to improve your physical condition. Often this involves basics like better sleep, better eating and more exercise. This isn't a health book, but we will be looking at ways to achieve this with a particular view to stress management – for instance, finding ways to exercise that don't bore you to death.

There are also physical controls that go beyond basic health improvements. Many find massage particularly effective. Aromatherapy may not be entirely proven, but there are enough people who do feel a benefit (and bearing in mind the nature of stress, the perception of benefit is enough) to make it worthwhile trying. Although we tend to think of stress as very much an internal thing, we shouldn't ignore these physical aids.

EMOTIONAL CONTROL

A large degree of our response to stress is dependent on our emotional state and self-image. If we are depressed and unhappy, stress will have a disproportionately large impact. We've all been in the position of snapping at someone for a very minor offence when we are already feeling miserable. Help with your emotional state can make all the difference to how you cope with stress.

Similarly, as we have already seen, self-confidence and feeling in control of your life are immensely valuable when it comes to fending off negative stress. Something as apparently flimsy as attitude and self-esteem has a very big impact. One of the strands you will find in the techniques is looking at building your self-esteem.

It's because of the importance of being in control that the apparent level of stress in a job isn't always a good indicator of the impact it will have on the individual. People with apparently stressful careers – company directors, successful self-employed people, surgeons, air traffic controllers – are much less likely to succumb to stress-related illness than those with apparently low-stress jobs. It's because production line workers or cleaners have so little control and hence much less self-esteem that they are more susceptible to stress. Appropriate emotional control can be a lifesaver.

SPIRITUAL CONTROL

There's a dichotomy in our world. We have never been more rational, scientific and analytical. Yet everyone will at some time feel a yearning for something more, something beyond the everyday. This need for something more has led to a huge interest in everything from New Age philosophy to established religions.

The specific approach taken isn't really of concern here, although there are several different suggestions in the techniques. The important consideration is the power of having a spiritual dimension to your life in helping to control stress. Many religions stress prayer or meditation as a means of building spiritual calm, which has the practical effect of reducing the impact of stress. In fact, properly used, such spiritual tools can be the most effective stress relievers, as they can be used in any circumstances and have a very powerful effect. Accepting a spiritual dimension to your life can also help to overcome difficulties with 'the big issues' that are rarely thought about or discussed in ordinary life, so remain a nagging worry on the threshold of consciousness.

STRESS DEFENCES

Sometimes, the best way to control stress is to avoid it ever reaching you. There are lots of good ways to reduce the impact of sitting in a traffic jam as you queue with the other commuters on the way to work, but it would be even better if you could avoid the queue in the first place. In this particular instance, defences might be anything from taking a different route to not commuting at all.

The natural temptation is to think that most of our stressors are inevitable. An example I've frequently used is an interview with a director of a large corporate, who bemoaned the fact that his work had made it impossible for him to see his children growing up. He thought that he had no choice. In fact, he had made a decision that his career and the level of personal wealth that went with it, was more important than his family life. It's not for me to say whether or not he made the right decision, but it was a decision, not an inevitable fact. Because the decision was never made consciously, we treat it as if it doesn't exist. That's a mistake. The same goes for stress factors. Often we assume that we can't avoid the stressors and so need controls to cope. Before reaching that stage, it's worth making the decisions that force the stressors on you visible rather than leaving them implicit.

KEEPING THE BALANCE

While building your personal resources against stress, bear in mind that your aim is not totally to eliminate stress from your life but to achieve a better balance. This is important to remember, both so you don't feel frustrated that you haven't achieved perfection and to avoid the inclination to remove positive stressors that drive you on to achieve success without endangering your health and happiness.

THIS BOOK

The techniques in *Instant Stress Management* are designed to help with different aspects of controlling stress reaction and defending yourself against stress. Each exercise is presented in a standard format, with brief details of any preparation required, running time, resources used and the timescale of its application, followed by a description of the exercise itself. Next come suggestions for feedback, comments on the outcome and possible variations on the technique. The final part of the entry is the star rating. This is a quick reference to show how the particular exercise provides physical control, emotional and/or spiritual control and defences – and how much fun it is likely to be. As much as possible, to keep with the 'instant' theme, the exercises require minimal preparation, but some exercises requiring a little more work beforehand are included as they can sometimes be particularly effective. Note that timings are a minimum – you can take longer over most of the exercises if it is appropriate.

How you use the exercises very much depends on your approach to life. There is nothing wrong with working through the whole book in sequence. Alternatively, the tables in the Appendix offer a number of ways of picking an exercise. There is a random selection table as a way of dipping into the exercises without getting into a rut. And there are tables arranging the exercises by how well they scored in the various star ratings. Use the exercises however they best fit with your schedule with the proviso that stress management requires regular practice. By using *Instant Stress Management* in bite-sized chunks, you are much more likely to be able to do something about your stress.

4

EXERCISES 1: ASSESSING

4.1 Control freaks

Preparation None.
Running time 15 minutes.
Resources Notepad.
Frequency Once.

The degree to which you are in control of your life, both in and out of work, can have a major impact on your stress levels. Take a sheet of paper and divide it into three columns: work, evenings and weekends (if you work shifts, change the headings accordingly). Spend a few minutes listing the major activities that you do in each column. Remember to include 'crossover' activities like commuting – it doesn't matter where.

Now, think yourself into each activity. How much do you feel in control? (Your perception is the most important thing here.) How much can you decide what to do when? Does your input matter, or are you following a pattern set by someone else? Are you following rules or interpreting principles? Note that time is a major factor in control. A deadline that is prepared for doesn't take control away from you. A deadline that is dropped on you at a moment's notice, or which you don't prepare for, can be debilitating. Label each activity H (high), M (medium) or L (low) for the level of control you have.

Feedback Note the low-control areas for positive action. Think about each of them. Are there any where it is possible to take more control? Can you deal with the stress arising using any of the principal categories you'll find in the next section: physical control (exercise, drugs, etc), mental control (thinking in a different way etc), spiritual control (achieving calm through spiritual means, etc) or defence (taking action to avoid the stressor reaching you)? Time management is also a very positive force for putting more control in your hands. See Chapter 6 for some recommended time management books.

Outcome As with all the techniques in this chapter, the outcome is not a final result, but a direction to consider when using the next chapter. Keep your list of low-control areas as a stimulus for use in future exercises.

Variations None. Unlike Chapter 5, these exercises are not given star ratings as they aren't appropriate.

4.2 The big stuff

Preparation None.
Running time 10 minutes.
Resources Notepad.
Frequency Once.

Big events in your life, whether positive or negative, are stressful. This exercise looks at what you have been through in the last year or so and are likely to go through this year. Spend a few minutes noting events that fit into each of these categories.

- Very high: death of close person, divorce or separation, jail or major injury.
- High: marriage, job loss, retirement, serious illness, pregnancy, birth, adoption, sexual problems, major change in financial status, death of friend, lots of arguments.
- Medium: large loan, debt, change in responsibilities at work, child leaving home, family disputes, change in home conditions.
- Low: other big events and stressors including holidays, parking tickets, etc.

Feedback This scale is a simplification of the life crisis table developed by Holmes and Rahe. They give each potential stress item a detailed score. All we are trying to do here is get a feel for the amount of pressure from major events. Note that isolated events of this kind do not pose a great threat to your overall stress levels. It is sustained stress that causes the damage – and this could come either from chronic minor stressors or from a series of major events (or both).

Outcome The major events will provide particular stress points and contribute to your overall levels of stress. Having a feel for whether you are in a period with a high level of major stressors will help you to decide whether you need to concentrate initially on defence – which really only works against minor stressors – or control.

Variations None.

4.3 How do you react?

Preparation None.
Running time Five minutes.
Resources Notepad.
Frequency Once.

We all have different ways of reacting to pressure, but broadly all these approaches fit into two categories, which were given the labels Type A and Type B by the American doctor Meyer Friedman in the 1960s. Spend a few minutes thinking which of these behaviours best fits your typical reaction to a situation. Try to be honest.

Type A	**Type B**
Find other people get in the way	Like working with other people
Feel on edge a lot	Usually feel laid back
Have angry outbursts	Take things calmly
Think failure is a major problem	Forgive failure easily
Hold in emotions	Let emotions go
Always trying to achieve more	Comfortable with the way things are
Find life a constant struggle	Find life generally easy
Like to work to deadlines	Like to work without deadlines

Feedback While Type A behaviour is more likely to lead to stress-related illness, it is also associated with getting things done. Often those who get to the top in their jobs will have some Type A characteristics. The problem, as always with stress, is not a simple one. It's also true that there is nothing harder to do than to change a reaction that is based on your personality. It is possible – and stress management techniques can help – but if you are naturally more inclined to Type A, you will find it difficult to move towards a balance with Type B.

Outcome By being aware of your position you can decide how (and if) you need to try to move the balance between Type A and Type B. Remember that this is not a black-and-white decision – you aren't trying to convert from Type A to Type B, but to achieve a healthy balance.

Variations None.

4.4 Emotion log

Preparation None.
Running time One week.
Resources Notepad.
Frequency Once.

An instant activity that lasts a week? But the time you take doing it will be negligible. In good Star Trek fashion, keep a log of what's going on and how you feel. It probably makes sense to divide this into four columns – what you are doing, how you feel about it, what you are thinking and how you are behaving. If you find it difficult to distinguish between thinking and feeling, just write across the two columns, but often we can distinguish between our logical, reasoned reaction and gut feel.

Feedback Look back over your week. Are there particular circumstances you found stressful? Note them. Look for activities that seem stressful or behaviour that is frenetic, out of control and negative. Look for thinking that is negative and destructive.

Outcome The purpose of this log is to get a feel for the danger points in your schedule – the activities and interactions that will cause you the most stress. With a map of the hot spots, you should be better able to apply your stress management toolkit.

Variations You can undertake this activity either on a regular basis (hourly, quarter day or whatever), or, probably better, at the breaks between activities. If you don't have breaks between activities, we've already identified a problem area – force some for this week. You might see extra benefit (see *Breaks*, 5.10). If jotting your log down is impractical, go even more Star Trek and use a pocket recorder.

4.5 Physical checks

Preparation None.
Running time Five minutes.
Resources Notepad.
Frequency Once.

Just how stressed are you right now? This is the first of two activities to check out the sorts of reactions that stress typically induces. Are you subject to several of these physical symptoms?

- Regular indigestion.
- Inability to sleep well.
- Aches and pains that respond to massage.
- Eczema, spots and other skin complaints.
- Frequent headaches.
- Always catching minor infections.
- Difficulty catching your breath.
- Feeling dizzy or shaky.
- Breaking out in a cold sweat.
- Tingling in your palms.

Feedback Note that not all physical symptoms of these kinds are caused by stress. If you have symptoms that continue, check with your doctor.

Outcome This exercise and the next are simply to help you to establish how much you are already in a state of chronic stress. They provide helpful background to stress management.

Variations None.

4.6 Emotional and spiritual checks

Preparation None.
Running time Five minutes.
Resources Notepad.
Frequency Once.

Stress reactions aren't limited to the physical – after all, stress is irritatingly holistic. This second activity of looking at typical stress symptoms considers the effects on your emotion, mind and spirit. How many, if any, of these sound familiar?

- Forgetting things a lot.
- Decision-making is difficult.
- Your driving has deteriorated.
- You feel restless.
- You get frustrated with others.
- Unusual impatience.
- Mood swings.
- Lack of concentration.
- Everything seems pointless.
- You can't keep on top of things.
- You feel defensive.

Feedback As with physical symptoms, bear in mind that many of these reactions can be due to illness as well as to pure stress. Don't hesitate to get medical advice if it is appropriate.

Outcome These checks are simply to help you to establish how much you are already in a state of chronic stress. They provide helpful background to stress management.

Variations None.

4.7 Depressed?

Preparation None.
Running time 10 minutes.
Resources Notepad.
Frequency Once.

Depression is more than just a matter of feeling miserable, it is a clinical condition. Confusingly, depression comes in two forms – it can be driven by outside events, or come from within. The latter case, where there seems to be no obvious cause, is a pure medical condition requiring attention. Look out for some of these possible indicators:

- Always feeling tired, however much sleep you get.
- Feeling worthless and without value.
- Loss of appetite.
- Problems managing at work (where previously this wasn't the case).
- Always feeling sad or simply blank.
- Unusual consideration of death.
- Anxiety without any real cause.
- Lack of interest in social life or sex.
- Can't put two thoughts together.

Feedback Although stress management techniques may help to relieve the depression that comes from outside events, it can't help the internal form. Make sure that depression isn't a part of the problem if you feel stressed – if in doubt, and the symptoms persist, contact your doctor.

Outcome In many cases depression is simply a reaction to stress, but it is important to recognize that this may not be the case so that alternative action can be taken.

Variations None.

4.8 Life lottery

Preparation None.
Running time 10 minutes.
Resources Pen and paper.
Frequency Occasionally.

Divide a sheet of paper in two. Jot down the main activities you undertake – between 10 and 20 – on one half of the paper. Don't differentiate between work and social activities – list everything significant. Trying not to be modest, highlight those you do well. Which have you had positive feedback about? Also extend back along the timeline. What did you do years ago that you were good at, but haven't done since? Similarly, think yourself into the future. Is there anything that you've never actually done, but think you would be good at? This is not a matter of impossible dreams, but talents you feel you may well have, given the chance.

Now the fun bit. Imagine you have come into a huge sum of money. You will never have to work again. Take a minute to enjoy the thought and its immediate implications. In the other half of the paper, draw up three columns: 'Yes', 'No' and 'New'. Assign all your activities to one of the first two columns. What would you do anyway? What would you instantly dismiss?

With the first two columns filled in, consider the third. Given the freedom provided by your riches, what else would you do? Try to be realistic, considering your talents, but be happy to stretch yourself.

Feedback Variants on this exercise have appeared in more books that I've written than any other. Sorry if this means you've several copies of it – but I'm unrepentant. This simple exercise is one of the most valuable you can do, whether you are trying to reduce stress, sort out time management or decide on your career direction.

Outcome Getting a clearer picture of just what it is that you want to be doing can be the first step in clearing away many stresses. Until you have clear objectives, it is very difficult to understand just what it is that is frustrating you.

Variations There are various other means of assessing your personal goals. If this doesn't work for you, hunt out some more – but this is usually effective. Repeat the exercise on an infrequent basis, particularly if major changes in your life are on the horizon.

4.9 More than tangible

Preparation None.
Running time 10 minutes.
Resources Pen and paper.
Frequency Occasionally.

This is a companion exercise to *Life lottery* (4.8), looking at the less tangible aspects of your needs and wants. First, think of relationships and emotions. Spend a couple of minutes jotting down what you want to get out your relationships – friends, partner, children, other family – and what you want to give. How would you like your social life to be? Then look at the current state of affairs. Jot down what things are really like. Now consider what's in between. Explore the obstacles that are preventing you from immediately achieving your ideal.

Undertake a parallel exercise for your spiritual and religious side, though with a slightly different approach. Spend a moment jotting down just what you believe in (in a spiritual sense) – give it a little time, it's not something we often think about. Next note your areas of uncertainty. What (within this area) do you wish you knew more about? Then look for any islands of peace in your life that you might not consciously think of as spiritual. Could any of these form a seed from which you might develop something into your areas of uncertainty? Finally, consider any of the spiritual supports available to you, from organized religion to New Age philosophy. It's probably best to start with something you have a cultural connection to, but set yourself a first direction to explore.

Feedback This represents the 'soft' side of the more practical *Life lottery*. It doesn't mean that it's unimportant, though. Good relationships, positive emotions and spiritual peace can be great defences against stress, just as the negatives in all these areas can be a great cause of stress.

Outcome This exercise won't fix your relationships or give you religion – but it will give you some directions to consider.

Variations As with the lottery exercise, there are plenty of other ways of looking at these big issues. This is just a start.

4.10 Are you assertive?

Preparation None.
Running time Five minutes.
Resources Notepad.
Frequency Once.

Being assertive is a great defence against stress. Imagine yourself in these three positions. In each case, jot down what you would do.

1. You are in the middle of a queue, having waited for half an hour. A young couple come along and casually walk into the queue right in front of you.
2. You have just bought a new CD-player. It didn't work, so you took it back. The replacement broke after the first week. When you take that back, the shop manageress says she won't replace the player, but will send it off to be repaired.
3. A child you are looking after for the afternoon demands some sweets, but you had been asked not to give him any.

Feedback There were a number of options in each case. You could fail to stand up for yourself, pretending that the situation hasn't happened. Or you can steam in aggressively and demand to get your way. Or you can be assertive, making it plain what is right without being threatening. For example, in the second scenario, an assertive person would refuse to accept anything other than a replacement, but with good grace and without losing his or her temper. There's also a fourth way that children are particularly good at – sly indirection. In taking this approach, you get someone else to take the blame, or manipulate those involved without actually demanding anything. Although this approach can get results, it can be damaging long-term to your reputation.

Note the distinction between assertiveness and aggression. Assertiveness may push the bounds of conventional politeness, but it is a calculated practical approach to reach an end. Aggression is an emotional response that usually has a negative effect on reaching a conclusion.

Outcome Some of the exercises in the next chapter will build assertiveness as part of your defence against stress – the point now is simply to decide how assertive you already are.

Variations None.

5

EXERCISES 2: DESTRESSING

5.1 Little successes

Preparation None.
Running time Two minutes.
Resources None.
Frequency Several times.

Self-esteem is an important contributory factor to stress and stress management. If your self-esteem is low, you are much more likely to succumb to stress-related illness. One of the undermining factors that keep self-esteem low is the diminishing spiral that says 'I never achieve anything', so you feel bad about not achieving, so you get stressed and achieve even less.

This is a very quick exercise that can have a surprisingly powerful effect on self-esteem. Spend a couple of minutes jotting down a handful of small achievements you have made in the day. However bad a day you've had, you should be able to find something positive to say – force yourself to generate at least three; don't take no for an answer. Repeat this exercise each day for a week or two.

Feedback Stick to small achievements for this exercise. We will look at stress-relief out of bigger achievements in a different topic (*I did that*, 5.40). No one is going to have a big achievement every day, but we all have a series of small achievements that will prove the fictional nature of the destructive view that everything about your life is terrible and you never succeed at anything.

Outcome It might seem that such a small success – it might just be 'I got to work on time' or 'I told my children a bed-time story' – is small beer compared to your problems. It doesn't matter; much of the stress from lack of self-esteem derives from an imagined bleak picture that 'everything' goes wrong for you. Realistically this can't be true – and proving it to yourself can really help.

Variations You could do this on a day-by-day basis, or (perhaps better) accumulate a list of all the little plusses across the period of time you are running the exercise.

Physical control	✪
Emotional/spiritual control	✪✪✪✪
Defence	✪
Fun	✪✪✪

5.2 Handling confrontation

Preparation None.
Running time 10 minutes.
Resources None.
Frequency Once.

Several techniques in *Instant Stress Management* relate to assertiveness and confrontation. This is probably the simplest but the most generally applicable. Having an argument is fine, but when neither side is listening to the other you end up with pointless confrontation. There are often better ways of reaching an outcome (see *Coherent discussion*, 5.42), but once you have got to confrontation, action is necessary.

Spend a couple of minutes jotting down what your first steps would be in these two confrontational positions. What would you say? How would you react, both physically and verbally?

1. A colleague comes in and starts prodding you, saying you've stolen their best member of staff.
2. A customer is complaining that your product or service has delayed them so they have missed an important meeting and what are you going to do about it? He is shouting.

Feedback It's tempting to ask the other person to calm down, but this often results in more anger. Don't tense up, and avoid the body language of tension. Don't laugh or smile (a common nervous reaction) – look sympathetic. Nod a lot. Keep your body open (don't fold your arms across your chest or scrunch down away from the person). Your first words should be in agreement. There will usually be some fact you can sympathize with. Continue positively but unthreateningly to say why you can't actually deliver entirely on their expectation. Finish by saying 'and I'm sure we can…' or whatever. End with an action that might be acceptable to both of you, using the linking 'and' to make sure it's building on what has gone before, not arguing with it.

Outcome Defusing confrontation is a good defence against stress. Try it out.

Variations Look out for other techniques in books on assertiveness.

Physical control	✪
Emotional/spiritual control	✪✪✪
Defence	✪✪✪✪
Fun	✪✪

5.3 Don't bury yourself

Preparation None.
Running time 10 minutes.
Resources Diary.
Frequency Once.

Almost everyone is guilty of procrastination. We put off the evil day when we have to make a decision. We put to one side the problem that is hanging over us because it is too unpleasant to deal with. We avoid giving someone bad news. The result is that we have a constant, nagging worry stressing us from within. Because of the way the brain works, any such nagging concern is likely to keep resurfacing, disrupting the other things that we need to do.

Spend a few minutes thinking through your personal goals and requirements. Do you have any nagging worries at the moment? Are there decisions that you really need to make, or actions that simply have to be taken? You can't do all these in 10 minutes, but you can decide when you are going to do them and make a note to remind yourself. Just the action of planning when you will do something removes a lot of the associated stress.

Feedback Do not confuse procrastination with living for today. Although, of course, you need to plan and there's nothing wrong with enjoying your past, the only point you can actually live is now. If you are constantly thinking of the future you are totally missing out – and building up stress. Living for today implies that you don't worry about lots of things that might be. Yes, plan and take action, but then forget the future until it is necessary to take action. This is quite different from procrastination, where you are constantly worrying about which action to take, but never actually doing anything.

Outcome Avoid procrastination and the stress that is its inevitable baggage – but remember to live for the day.

Variations None.

Physical control	✪
Emotional/spiritual control	✪✪✪
Defence	✪✪✪✪
Fun	✪✪

5.4 Capture ideas

Preparation None.
Running time Two minutes.
Resources Notebook.
Frequency Regularly.

Ideas are strange things, popping up at the most unlikely times and places. People have them in the car, in the bath, while walking, while sitting dreaming in a field, on the toilet, in bed… but hardly ever at the desk (and certainly not under pressure).

Leaving ideas uncollected is a bad move. Not only do you miss out on your inspirational gems, it generates stress. You will try to hold the ideas in memory. So for the next few hours you will be muttering 'I just need to remember X', or 'What was that idea, now?' Because idea generation often happens in the mental state between waking and dreaming, it's easy for the detail of an idea to fade quickly. Leave it longer and you may still be trying to remember the idea as you go to sleep, disturbing your night. And you may forget it entirely.

Carry a notebook, small enough to keep in your pocket. When an idea occurs, jot it down. On a regular basis – at least weekly – revisit your notebook and turn worthwhile ideas into tasks.

Feedback Inevitably ideas will strike when you haven't got your notebook, or can't use it. Leaving yourself a message can help. Call your voicemail (handy in the car if you've a hands-free phone), and leave a message about the idea. Or borrow someone's e-mail and send yourself a note.

Outcome Capturing ideas provides the triple benefits of the idea itself, of not clogging up mental resources trying to remember the idea (always stressful) and of not being frustrated by losing an idea.

Variations Some people find a pocket recorder more effective than a notebook. It certainly means that you can capture ideas easily while driving. I find the notebook better, because I'm more likely to do something with the output – but try a recorder if it sounds sensible.

Physical control	✪
Emotional/spiritual control	✪✪✪
Defence	✪✪✪✪
Fun	✪✪

5.5 Stress workout

Preparation None.
Running time 15 minutes.
Resources Notepad.
Frequency Once.

Regular exercise is not just good for your health, it is an essential part of a stress-reduction programme. This section isn't about exercising – that takes two or more sessions a week of at least half an hour – it's about planning. Most people who suddenly decide to take exercise don't keep it up. Try this three point plan.

1. Self-motivation. Find a driving reason to exercise (go for the gut, like staying alive for your children). Make sure it is at the forefront of your mind when you decide how to use your time.
2. Choose something you enjoy. This may seem self-evident, but many people choose a form of exercise that's trendy (the gym) or that's career boosting (golf). Find something you really enjoy.
3. Add value. Get together with friends and make it a social event, or choose an activity where you can wear a Walkman and listen to music, speech radio, book tapes or learn a language.

Feedback Your activity should be aerobic, maximizing use of the body. Typical choices are swimming, cycling, running or gym routines – avoid sports that don't involve continuous activity. If, like me, you find these boring, don't ignore walking. We're used to walking as a gentle stroll to introduce us to exercise. In fact, walking quickly can be an effective exercise (especially if hills are involved) with less risk of damage than jogging. What's more, walking is practical. I hate exercise for its own sake – having a goal of getting somewhere doubles the value. Plunging into heavy exercise is not good for you. Get some guidance if you are in any doubt.

Outcome Exercise reduces physical tension and brings down levels of stress chemicals. It builds up the body, helps general fitness and ability to cope. The physical control of stress is the foundation on which everything else is built. You can't overlook this one.

Variations None.

Physical control	✪✪✪✪
Emotional/spiritual control	✪✪
Defence	✪✪
Fun	✪✪

5.6 Environmental stuff

Preparation Meeting.
Running time 30 minutes.
Resources Notepad.
Frequency Once.

Most people spend between 30 and 60 hours a week in their working environment. That's a long time – it's probably more, for instance, than you spend in your lounge at home. Consider the relative amount of effort you put into making your lounge a pleasant environment and into making your workplace pleasant.

Get together the people who work in a separable chunk of your workplace (see Variations if you work alone). Put up two flip charts. On one, list everything that's wrong with your present workplace environment – small and large. On the other, list anything you feel makes for a pleasant environment – again cover small detail as much as large-scale considerations.

Now, combining the two, come up with the top 10 things you can do in terms of 'bangs per buck' that would make the environment more pleasant. These can be individually or across the group. Finally, consider where you can get the money from, and put together a timetable for making them happen.

Feedback The money bit can be a stumbling block. The company may contribute, but consider whether the employees should contribute too – wouldn't it be worth it? Often a bigger problem is bureaucracy that, for example, doesn't allow individual decoration or changes to the workplace. Consider the options of defeating the bureaucracy (see *Bureaucratic bounce-back*, 5.34, for some more general approaches), cheating or ignoring the rules (subject to safety considerations) – but get something done.

Outcome The conditions in which you work influence your stress levels, positively or negatively. Most employers are clued up enough about stress to realize this and to be supportive. Be prepared to fight designer uniformity to get a pleasant working environment.

Variations If you don't work with others, perform the exercise anyway – your environmental concerns are just as great. You have the advantage of less need to agree with others over what you do, but may find it harder to get funding.

Physical control	✪✪✪✪
Emotional/spiritual control	✪✪
Defence	✪✪
Fun	✪✪✪

5.7 Laugh!

Preparation None.
Running time Five minutes.
Resources Notebook.
Frequency Once.

Stress can get into a feedback loop. The more stressed you are, the more unhappy you become. This unhappiness then results in further stress. A fundamental requirement is to break out of that loop, and a very powerful tool for managing this is laughter.

Spend a few minutes putting together a laughter lifeline pack. Note down everything you can think of that makes you laugh. Not a snide, put-down sort of laugh. In fact, not any nasty or calculated sort of laughter, but sheer, uncontrolled hilarity. It could be certain books, cartoon strips, films, comedians, TV programmes – or just a good evening out with your friends. Once you've got your list, see if you can have one or two laughter lifeline elements on call for when you feel down.

Feedback We don't find it at all strange that we are required by law to keep first-aid kits on hand in case someone needs some minor physical repairs, so it's rather odd that we don't give any consideration to our mental well-being. Humour and laughter tend to be frowned on in a business context. Apparently we aren't supposed to enjoy ourselves when we are working. This sheer madness seems to derive from some Victorian work ethic, or the strange concept that humour and laughter are somehow not professional. Whatever the cause, it needs fighting.

Outcome Laughter is a multiple stress reliever, helping on the mental, physical and spiritual level. There are actual chemical processes at work that partly explain this, but a lot of it is down to the benefits of sheer enjoyment. Indulge!

Variations This is a particularly good technique to apply when others are suffering from stress. Get them involved in an evening of laughter. A trip to see a top-rate comedian performing is probably best of all. There's something very refreshing about laughing with a group of other people.

Physical control	✪✪✪
Emotional/spiritual control	✪✪✪✪
Defence	✪✪
Fun	✪✪✪✪

5.8 Unloading

Preparation None.
Running time Five minutes.
Resources None.
Frequency Daily.

Your short-term memory can only handle about seven items. This is why it is so difficult to hold onto a telephone number you have just looked up. We only keep it in short-term memory by grouping numbers together, perhaps by considering the dialling code as a single unit. The same restriction applies to a list of tasks. If you try to keep everything you need to do today in your head there will be a horrible juggling act going on, as the different tasks fight for the seven or so slots of your immediate attention. At the extreme, you can get into a state similar to that of a computer with insufficient memory. It spends increasing amounts of time transferring information to and from disk. In the end this activity takes up almost all the time – a condition that is referred to as thrashing. Most of us have been in this state where almost all your thoughts are taken up with trying to get your mental list straight.

There is only one answer – commit the list to paper (or whiteboard, or computer). Put together the day's basic action list, with any outstanding tasks on a side list to make sure they don't get lost. This is not a major scheduling exercise – it should only take minutes.

Feedback Some people are natural list makers; others find lists restricting. If you fall into the second camp, you will find this exercise quite difficult. It will be easy to find something else to do instead. Fight the urge. This list will benefit even you.

Outcome This is a simple activity with surprisingly good leverage on stress levels. Do it.

Variations Conventional wisdom has it that the evening before is the best time to make a task list. However, if your mind is clearest in the morning you might find first thing better. If so, make sure that you make the list early enough to cope with any logistics arising.

Physical control	✪✪✪✪
Emotional/spiritual control	✪✪
Defence	✪
Fun	✪✪

5.9 You are what you eat

Preparation None.
Running time 15 minutes.
Resources None.
Frequency Once.

There's no magic link between food and stress relief, but being broadly healthy is a positive factor in stress management, and diet is a contributory factor to health. While there are constant arguments about some specifics of diet – do eggs increase cholesterol? Are vegetables better raw or heavily boiled? – some aspects are very clear. The fact that most of us should reduce our intake of saturated fat and salt, while eating more vegetables, fruit, fish, fibre and (surprising to some) carbohydrates is hard to dispute. Similarly, most of us ought to drink more water, especially if we are under stress when we are more likely to become dehydrated.

Spend a few minutes thinking about your diet. Identify a handful of changes that would improve your diet. Think about how you could implement these changes. For example, if you wanted to eat more fruit and vegetables, could you take a carrot and an apple to work for when you get peckish? Often the reason we don't eat 'better' food is that it's too much trouble – make it easy instead.

Feedback Being careful about your diet can actually be stressful. Most of us don't find dieting particularly enjoyable, and at times it is a positive pain. Unless you have medical reasons for sticking to a diet, be prepared to break it infrequently but quite regularly as a treat, to celebrate and to unwind. Similarly, a regular if controlled amount of alcohol, particularly red wine, isn't a bad idea unless you have associated medical problems. Although alcohol is actually a stimulant, many people find a moderate amount of alcoholic drink helpful in the process of unwinding.

Outcome An improvement in diet (and hence physical condition) and a reduction in the stress caused by worrying about health issues should be the twin outcomes here.

Variations None.

Physical control	✪✪✪✪
Emotional/spiritual control	✪✪
Defence	✪
Fun	✪✪

5.10 Breaks

Preparation None.
Running time Five minutes.
Resources None.
Frequency Once.

We've all been in the situation. You are working under pressure. Time is short and there is a huge amount to be done. So you work long into the night, steaming open your eyelids with cups of coffee, hardly stopping. Stress grows and grows as the deadline grows near.

Unfortunately there is overwhelming evidence that this is not a great way to get the most out of your brain. The amount of information retained and the quality of your output drops off after time working at the same task. By taking a series of short breaks, much more can be achieved. There isn't a magic length for the chunks of time, but most people find between 15 minutes and an hour, with breaks of around five minutes will overcome the deterioration.

In the few minutes allowed for this exercise, you aren't going to get anything practical done. Instead, take a task you have ahead (or invent one for the exercise) and rough out a schedule of chunks and breaks. Then make sure you use your schedule.

Feedback It's very tempting to carry on if everything is going smoothly. But however well it seems things are going, your ability to remember and to reason will benefit from breaks. The break should be something completely different, involving a different use of the mind. Getting out in the fresh air for a few minutes and unwinding is ideal.

Outcome Breaking things into chunks makes a lot of sense, but it's human nature to forge on and try to get through, especially under pressure. It often takes tight scheduling to force yourself to take breaks to begin with – but persevere for improved output and less stress.

Variations Try different chunkings to see which works best for you. The natural tendency is to try for the longest chunks as these seem more efficient. It isn't necessarily the case that they will be best for you.

Physical control	✪✪✪✪
Emotional/spiritual control	✪✪✪
Defence	✪✪✪
Fun	✪✪

5.11 Rage

Preparation None.
Running time Two minutes.
Resources None.
Frequency Occasionally.

Rage is everywhere in the media. It might be that old favourite road rage, or newer manifestations like PC rage or airport rage. In fact, according to recent studies, rage is nothing new, but something insidious is happening. The media's use of the label has made us all conscious of the existence of the phenomenon. And like it or not, that label has given rage a certain legitimacy. These outbursts are somehow more acceptable because we know what is causing them.

Generally, rage results from over-stimulation. Driving is a classic example, where there is a constant underlying stress brought about by the need to concentrate on the road and cope with busy traffic. This leaves the driver too near the edge, ready to be pushed into a major stress reaction by a small incident.

Such rage is bad for both your health and your performance. If you feel anger welling up, take a couple of slow breaths and put the matter into context. For instance, when someone pulls in front of you while driving, think how trivial this would be on the pavement – why is it different in a car? Don't get angry, laugh at them. Imagine the other driver sitting on the toilet. Mock their vehicle. Alternatively, put yourself in the other person's position. This can be particularly useful in circumstances like delays at an airport. The poor person at the information desk hasn't caused the delay – why get angry with them? Think how they must feel. Finally think of your own benefit. You'll get a better response if you are nice – don't rage, smile. Smiles are the enemies of thoughtless rage.

Feedback It's easy enough to write these logical steps, and another to use them when you want to tear someone's head off, or smash your PC. It takes determination and staying power to beat rage.

Outcome The benefits to your blood pressure and general stress levels far outweigh the cost of being disciplined enough to conquer rage.

Variations None.

Physical control	✪✪
Emotional/spiritual control	✪✪✪✪
Defence	✪✪✪✪
Fun	✪✪

5.12 Touchy-smelly

Preparation None.
Running time 15 minutes.
Resources None.
Frequency Occasionally.

Massage has long been seen as a way of soothing stress. Whether used on its own or in combination with aromatherapy, it has a lot going for it. Like exercise, it helps the blood flow and relaxes over-tightened muscles. How you get your massage is up to you. You can give yourself some basic massages – scalp, neck, shoulders – while bringing in a friend with a suitable book should enable you to get considerably further. There's no doubt, though, that having a massage from a professional will produce the best results, especially as experienced hands will often be able to feel where the muscles are most in need of work.

Aromatherapy does not require massage, although the two work together well. Just breathing in the appropriate essence, or perhaps taking an appropriately scented warm (but not hot) bath can be effective on its own. You should be safe in do-it-yourself mode with commercial aromatherapy products, but it's worth taking advice if you venture into the heavy-duty oils used by professionals.

Feedback Like most alternative methods, aromatherapy has a mixed press. There certainly seems to be something in it. For example, British Airways is now providing lavender oil in its First Class wash bags. There seems some evidence that a quick squirt of this on the pillow aids sleep – a very direct help in stress management. Other claims are less well supported, but this has to be an area where the recommendation is to try it and see. Stress is such a complex mix of the mental and the physical that what works for you is what matters, whether or not this is for physical or psychological reasons.

Outcome There's an essence of pure relaxation about massage, and aromatherapy for some makes it even more effective. If you are having trouble relieving stress, especially with associated physical tenseness, it is well worth trying either or both.

Variations None.

Physical control	✪✪✪✪
Emotional/spiritual control	✪✪✪
Defence	✪
Fun	✪✪✪

5.13 Ritual relaxation

Preparation None.
Running time Five minutes.
Resources None.
Frequency Once.

Ritual, a regular practice, is a powerful bulwark against stress. An established ritual for a small portion of each day provides an anchor for a fast-changing life.

In itself, the ritual doesn't have to be big or significant. And there are times when you will have to abandon it with good grace. But the norm should be that your ritual exists. Evenings are generally the best time, as the ritual helps you to refocus after the workday. It might be having 10 minutes with a glass of red wine, or reading a story to the children, or watching Coronation Street or attending Evensong – the activity is less important than the ritual nature.

Sit down for five minutes and think about your life. What elements are potential rituals? How can you protect them? Try to give yourself something daily, preferably in the evening. You might also like to establish a weekly ritual at the weekend – here the evening setting is less important, but again it needn't take up too much time. Try it for a few weeks to get in the swing.

Feedback Ritual has got a bad name. If you say 'It's a ritual with him', the tone is condescending. The implication is that having a regular pattern of doing things means being stuck in a rut. There's a germ of truth there. If everything you do has to fit a pattern, then you are doomed in today's ultra-paced, fast changing, scintillating world. But it's not that simple. No matter how flexible you are, you can benefit from a small core of ritual. Like the family and the home, it provides stability in an otherwise chaotic environment. Rituals mustn't dominate, but there should be a thread of them in your life.

Outcome Many of us already have a ritual but don't recognize it, and certainly don't give it the importance it deserves. Others currently lack an anchor and will benefit even more from this exercise.

Variations None.

Physical control	✪✪
Emotional/spiritual control	✪✪✪✪
Defence	✪✪
Fun	✪✪✪

5.14 Mentor mine

Preparation None.
Running time 15 minutes.
Resources Notepad.
Frequency Once.

There's lots you can do alone to manage stress, but sometimes you need a hand. This doesn't necessarily mean a therapist, though. Just having someone to talk through your problems and aspirations with is immensely valuable.

First spend five minutes thinking about your life, at work and at home. Jot down the most significant things that take up your time, your energy and your worrying. Then think through your contacts. An ideal mentor is:

- Absolutely trustworthy – you want to be able to discuss confidential matters.
- Someone you know well… but not a close friend.
- Someone who is good at listening.
- Someone you have regular contact with.

Don't approach your choice and say 'I want you to be my mentor', just start to get together with them infrequently but regularly and chat about what concerns you.

Feedback To be effective, you will need regular chats with your mentor. Don't try to make it formal. The whole point of a mentoring session is that it can cover anything and everything. Note, by the way, you have an unwritten obligation to act as a mentor too; there's someone out there who needs you to listen to them.

One warning: sometimes patients develop affection for an analyst of the opposite sex; because you are forcing yourself to be intimate with your mentor, there is a danger of getting mixed-up emotionally if you are dealing with someone you might find attractive.

Outcome The mentor's role is uniquely powerful in helping you to get to terms with stressing situations. Get one as soon as possible.

Variations None.

Physical control	✪
Emotional/spiritual control	✪✪✪✪
Defence	✪✪
Fun	✪✪✪

5.15 Stage fright

Preparation Requirement to give presentation.
Running time 15 minutes.
Resources None.
Frequency Occasionally.

Most of us have to speak to a large audience occasionally. For some it comes naturally, but for many it is a frightening experience. Next time you have a large presentation to give, use this planning exercise to counter that stress. As soon as you know you are presenting, put together a rough set of milestones. Something like: presentation ready, script ready, rehearsed, packed. Some of the stress with presentations comes long before the event – the more you are prepared, the less it will hover in your mind.

Several days before, run through the presentation in full. You may feel stupid standing in front of your PC talking to the air, but a run-through helps with timings and enables you to spot sections that need rewriting or don't work. If necessary, do this two or three times until your notes are just an occasional reference. It's fine to write a detailed prose script, by the way, but don't read it. Condense it down to keywords to use on the day.

When it comes to the event, explore the venue first if possible – it's less stressful to present in a familiar environment. Make sure the technology works (and you've got a backup in case it doesn't). Just before the presentation do a breathing exercise. Get yourself into a positive frame of mind. Smile a lot. Know it's going to succeed. Then go out and enjoy it. While presenting, scan the audience, but stick longer with the faces that give positive feedback.

Feedback Everyone who goes on stage gets butterflies in the stomach. Some professional actors suffer terribly from stage fright. Don't let this perfectly natural reaction turn to excessive stress. When you give a presentation you are acting. Act yourself into a positive role. Enjoy it – everyone can.

Outcome Presentations always involve stress, but by being appropriately prepared you can limit this to positive stress.

Variations None.

Physical control	✪✪
Emotional/spiritual control	✪✪✪
Defence	✪✪✪
Fun	✪✪

5.16 Pushing waves

Preparation Find a quiet place.
Running time Five minutes.
Resources None.
Frequency Occasionally.

Stand with your legs slightly apart and your knees unlocked (lock your knees in the vertical and then just relax them slightly out of this). Push your bottom backwards as if you had a large kangaroo tail that you were resting on behind you. Make sure that your back and shoulders are straight. Now, imagine a cord from the centre of your head to the ceiling. Let this pull your head up a little. Relax. Okay, that's the standing sorted out. Now hold your hands in front of you, fingers pointing upwards and palms away from you, with the backs of your hands against your chest and your elbows by your hips. Keeping your hands vertical, slowly push them away from you until your arms are almost outstretched but so that your elbows don't lock. Once they are out there, slowly pull them back towards you with your hands horizontal and the palms pointing downwards. Try this a few times until the movement is slow, graceful and wave-like. Make the transition at each end of the movement as smooth as you can. Now for the breathing. As you move your hands away from you, breathe out through your mouth. As you move your hands towards you, breathe in through your nose. Slow down the whole process so that your movements are as slow as your breathing can become. Close your eyes and continue with slow, graceful movements and slow deep breaths.

Feedback This is a Chi Gung exercise that is often used for relaxation in Tai Chi classes. It is mind-bogglingly simple, but extremely effective. Do try it; you will be surprised at how relaxed you feel.

Outcome Relaxation helps you to drain the physical impact of stress and to give yourself a chance to balance out the mental impact.

Variations Try different forms of relaxation to see which suits you best.

Physical control	✪✪✪✪
Emotional/spiritual control	✪✪✪
Defence	✪
Fun	✪✪✪

5.17 Breathing is good for you

Preparation Find a quiet place.
Running time Five minutes.
Resources None.
Frequency Regularly.

It's a self-evident truth that breathing is a good thing – but there's breathing and there's breathing. As all singers know, there are two types of breathing – with the chest muscles and with the diaphragm. The latter is more controlled and gives you a much deeper breath, yet it tends to be under-used, particularly by those under stress.

First, try to feel that diaphragmatic breathing. Stand up straight, but not tense. Take a deep breath and hold it for a second. Your chest will rise. Now try to keep your chest in the 'up position' while breathing in and out. You should feel a tensing and relaxing around the stomach area. Rest a hand gently on your stomach to feel it in action.

Now lie on the floor or sit comfortably in a chair. Close your eyes. Begin to breathe regularly: count up to five (in your head!) as you breathe in through your nose. Hold it for a second, then breathe out through your mouth, again counting to five. Rest a hand on your stomach. Don't consciously force your rib cage to stay up now, but concentrate on movement of the diaphragm. Your stomach should gently rise as you breathe in and fall as you breathe out.

Feedback One of the great things about breathing exercises like this is that they can be performed pretty well anywhere. For instance, although driving a car isn't the ideal position, you can still indulge in deep breathing.

Outcome A regular five-minute session of breathing properly will provide the foundation for many other stress management techniques. It is simple and very effective. What's more, it will help with your breath control if you sing or play a wind instrument.

Variations Don't miss out on this one – it involves little effort and it is very valuable. Ideally you should do it daily – some recommend breathing exercises as many as three times a day.

Physical control	✪✪✪✪
Emotional/spiritual control	✪✪
Defence	✪
Fun	✪✪

5.18 Low-stress travel

Preparation Travel requirement.
Running time Five minutes.
Resources None.
Frequency Regularly.

Travel can be stressful or enjoyable. With a little effort you can make things easier. If travelling by air or rail, book in advance. Carry the minimum – stick to hand luggage on a plane. Use trains if possible – the ability to move around freely, to work or read more comfortably all make the travel less stressful (assuming the train arrives on time). Make something of the travelling time – find ways to enjoy it. It seems accepted now that you can battle jet lag by avoiding traditional timings. So, for instance, when travelling across the Atlantic between the US and the UK, travel earlier in the day.

When scheduling a series of meetings involving travel be generous with timing. An early hold-up can produce knock-on delays throughout the day. Sometimes it is advantageous to cancel the second event of the day so the rest aren't disrupted. If you are delayed, use a mobile phone to alert the people ahead of you, and have plenty to do (physically or mentally) to make use of the time. Relaxing music and relaxation exercises help, but the best protection against travel time stress is acceptance. You are late; there is nothing you can do about it. It's a lot easier to write than to do, but it is possible and helps a lot.

Feedback For years when I went on a long-haul flight, people would make remarks like: 'It's nice work if you can get it', implying that it was a perk. In fact, I realized that for me long-haul travel was unpleasant. Since then I have found that it is often possible to get someone else to travel (or cancel the travel altogether), without any reduction in the quality of job. Sometimes business travel is necessary, but the occasions are fewer than you might imagine.

Outcome Travel wears you down – giving consideration to thc stress elements can help a lot.

Variations None.

Physical control	✪✪✪
Emotional/spiritual control	✪✪✪
Defence	✪✪✪
Fun	✪✪

5.19 It's good to talk

Preparation None.
Running time Five minutes.
Resources None.
Frequency Regularly.

When we are under pressure it's easy to see any interruption to your efforts as irritating but, in fact, small doses of regular social chat are beneficial. Apart from anything else, breaking your activity into chunks (see *Breaks*, 5.10) will result in less pressure and more efficiency. But the social aspect goes beyond improving the effectiveness of your output. Having positive social interaction (make sure it's not backbiting or moaning, which will increase stress) will act as a natural stress suppressor.

Have you had a chat this morning or afternoon? Make sure that you do.

Feedback When a company is under pressure there are sometimes panics about the amount of time spent on non-work activities in working time. The topic might be chatting or surfing the Web, but the response is usually the same – to get heavy about time (and hence money) wasted. It is a great tool for stress control and for good management if you can separate inputs and outputs. The company's measure of how well you are doing, and most particularly your personal measure, should be what you produce, not how many hours you spend at your desk.

Outcome Having a chat a couple of times a day helps to make sure you break up your work and acts as a stress suppressor, as long as the conversation is positive. Consider from this whether it would be helpful for you to put more focus on your outputs than your inputs.

Variations A phone call (or even a string of e-mails) is better than nothing, but you can't beat a face-to-face conversation.

Physical control	✪✪
Emotional/spiritual control	✪✪✪✪
Defence	✪✪
Fun	✪✪✪

5.20 Pat on the back

Preparation None.
Running time Two minutes.
Resources None.
Frequency Regularly.

Some of us are very good at giving other people a pat on the back when they've done something right – and that's an excellent thing to do, because with any luck they will return the compliment. Receiving regular small pats on the back stops the build up of the feeling that you aren't appreciated, and hence stress.

Sometimes, though, no one is going to do the back-patting for you. It might be that those who should be doing it are too busy, or simply aren't very good at telling people what a good job they've done (if that's the case, try to find ways to pat them on the back as a stimulus). It might be that there isn't anyone there to do it for you. If so, don't be shy about giving yourself a pat on the back.

When something goes well, shout 'Yes!' and punch the air, take yourself on a quick guided tour of the benefits, bask a brief while in the glory, perhaps buy yourself a little treat – anything from a chocolate bar, through to a nice lunch to the sort of toy that appeals to you.

Feedback Many of us are held back by the consideration that we can't be objective, and anyway we shouldn't be blowing our own trumpet. When there's no one else to do the trumpet blowing, don't be shy – much stress is conquered by being in control, and control includes the ability to enjoy your successes. See *Because I'm worth it* (5.35) for more on establishing self-worth.

Outcome This needn't be more than saying to yourself 'That went rather well' and indulging in the luxury of a big grin, but psychologically the impact is considerable. Give yourself a pat more often – you know you deserve it.

Variations None.

Physical control	✪✪
Emotional/spiritual control	✪✪✪✪
Defence	✪✪
Fun	✪✪✪✪

5.21 Don't do that

Preparation None.
Running time Five minutes.
Resources None.
Frequency Several times.

This one sounds bizarre, but give it a chance. Being negative is stress inducing. The more you shoot things down, criticize (in a destructive way) and put across negatives, the more you induce stress in yourself. It seems that the brain is pretty dumb and has difficulty distinguishing between mental and physical processes. The more you think and communicate in a negative manner, the more you will stress up.

Next time you are having an energetic conversation, take a step back and monitor those words. It's the obvious negatives (don't, no, stop), the commands (must, will, should, do this) and the put-downs (idiotic, stupid, brainless) that you need to trap. The more you use them, the more your brain becomes convinced you are moving into threat and activates the mechanisms of stress. This doesn't mean that you should agree with everything, but try to phrase and think in a more open way. Don't tell them they can't do X, ask them if they've thought of doing Y. Don't tell them they should do A, instead, point out that they could do A. Find things to compliment rather than to criticize.

Feedback Of course, you can't always avoid the negative. Apart from anything, phrasing everything positively would waste the richness of the English language. This exercise has a negatively phrased title – but I was prepared to take the stress for you. The point is rather to move the general feeling away from the negative into the positive. If it seems that this is being too soft on the other person involved, remember whose benefit this is for – yours. But you never know, you may get a more constructive outcome.

Outcome Negativity is a great way to stress yourself. By moving over to a more positive approach you can reduce this self-stressing – and probably get better results, too.

Variations This exercise is worth repeating several times until it becomes more natural.

Physical control	✪✪✪
Emotional/spiritual control	✪✪✪
Defence	✪
Fun	✪✪

5.22 Medicinal reading

Preparation None.
Running time 15 minutes.
Resources Books.
Frequency Daily.

I sometimes think books should be labelled 'To be taken twice a day, or when stress arises'. Under the right circumstances, reading books is very calming. This isn't a prescription to deal with peak stress. If you are extremely worried about something, or bursting for action, you will not be able to get into a book. But books are ideal for chronic stress, when the little things in life wear you down.

Most of us don't read enough – in breadth or quantity. Find two slots a day to do some reading. Then look at your choice of books. You need something that will take you away from everyday pressures. Don't go for a 'quality' novel about depressing people and their agonizing lives. The book doesn't have to be upbeat, but the last thing you want is to be depressed. Often genre fiction can be effective. After all, a fantasy or a murder is unlikely to reflect your everyday problems. Equally, readable non-fiction can work well. Look at areas like travel fiction, chatty business books (narrative books, rather than an action book like this) and business biographies, popular science or history.

Feedback There are many reasons for reading. Stress management is only one component. Sometimes, perhaps standing up on a crowded commuter train, reading passes the time without really doing anything about stress. To get the best stress relief you ought to be sitting in a comfortable chair with no disturbances.

Outcome Just because this technique is only applicable to the everyday accumulation of small stresses does not mean that it is trivial. Keep up that reading.

Variations Other media can be effective. Don't dismiss the TV and movies because they're down-market. Similarly, computer games can be good for stress relief. Adventure games have a similar effect to a novel, while an action game might push up the adrenalin levels temporarily, but it will be cathartic in taking out your stress on a clear, identifiable enemy.

Physical control	✪
Emotional/spiritual control	✪✪✪✪
Defence	✪✪
Fun	✪✪✪✪

5.23 Sulkers

Preparation None.
Running time Five minutes.
Resources Notepad; pen.
Frequency Once.

Sulking is a human reaction. We all do it to a degree. But some people can make it more than a few minutes of irritation. At the extreme, there are individuals who can bear a grudge for years. Such behaviour is less immediately stressful than aggression, but over time it will wear you down until it seems unbearable.

Spend five minutes jotting down what action you'd take if you had to deal with a sulker. If you actually work (or live) with someone like this, so much the better. Just having a plan can make a significant difference. Otherwise, because each thing the sulker does is very minor, it's easy to leave them in control. Here are a few tips that you might consider if they aren't already in your plan:

- Sulking is childish behaviour. Just as you would with a child, don't let anger take over, or sulk back at them. Ignore the sulks; be positive when they don't sulk.
- If you don't know why they are sulking, try to find out. It will take several tries, as a traditional component of sulking is denying there's anything wrong. Use *Broken record* (5.41).
- If you don't succeed in getting a reason out of them, explain that you can't help if they won't talk to you, so you'll just have to carry on as if it's not the case, but you are very willing to discuss it as and when they want to.
- Really do carry on regardless.

Feedback If you let sulkers get away with it for a long period of time, you are playing into their hands. They can, apparently reasonably, argue that you are over-reacting if you are being driven to distraction by little more than a subtlety of tone. Don't give them the weaponry.

Outcome Sulking seems trivial, but can evoke considerable stress if you are subjected to it over a long time. Counter it.

Variations None.

Physical control	✪
Emotional/spiritual control	✪✪
Defence	✪✪✪✪
Fun	✪✪

5.24 Hitting target

Preparation *Life lottery* (4.8).
Running time Five minutes.
Resources None.
Frequency Regularly.

Although it's possible to do this exercise on its own, it will work better if you have undertaken the *Life lottery* (4.8) exercise first. On a regular basis (perhaps quarterly), check your personal objectives. These should be a handful (certainly less than 10) of major achievements that you are aiming for at the moment. Some of them could be very long-term, others closer to home. Significantly more frequently (perhaps weekly), assess your current targets. These should be things you might expect to achieve in the next week or two.

Keep your targets and objectives somewhere highly visible. They will help you to deflect stress by concentrating your efforts on these key elements, and will be even more helpful if other people can see them. They can then understand what is important to you and may modify their behaviour accordingly. Don't fret too much if a target is missed, but if one keeps shifting, take a little time to see why and do something about it – don't have a target that moves back a week each week indefinitely.

Feedback As a technique this is fundamental time management. This worries some people, who think of time management as an over-bureaucratic system for people whose lives revolve around lists. There's no doubt that time management can become this, but the basic aspects of time management are central to getting control of your life, and hence managing your stress. Having clear personal targets is quite different from management by objective and other form-filling bureaucracy.

Performing the *Life lottery* (4.8) exercise first should help you to set your objectives and targets, as you will have a clearer idea of where you are trying to go.

Outcome Identifying practical targets for yourself, in combination with longer-term objectives, is a very effective counter to the sort of stress that eventually has you running in circles chasing your tail.

Variations See Chapter 6 for more information on practical time management.

Physical control	✪
Emotional/spiritual control	✪✪✪
Defence	✪✪✪✪
Fun	✪✪

5.25 Listen well

Preparation None.
Running time Five minutes.
Resources None.
Frequency Regularly.

Poor communication is a relentless generator of stress, and the area of communication most of us are worst at is listening. To improve your listening skills, start taking a step back from your conversations. On a regular basis, try to monitor just what is going on. First, make sure you are listening – really listening, not thinking about something else or what you are going to say. Use non-verbal cues to emphasize that you are listening. Lean forward, use eye contact, acknowledge that you've heard with 'hmm-hmm' noises. Try not to fidget or move around and play with things as you listen.

Strangely, it's also important to leave the person you are listening to with enough silence to fill. While they will benefit from your non-verbal cues, talking can sometimes get in the way. When there is a silence, don't rush in to fill it, however tempting it may be. Sometimes the person who is talking needs silence to assemble their thoughts. Give them a chance.

Finally, use your words to bring out their story. Use open questions to give them a chance to develop their topic rather than closed questions that force a 'yes' or 'no' answer. At appropriate points, echo what you think you've heard so that you can confirm that you really are communicating. And whatever you do, look interested.

Feedback This may seem artificial to begin with, which is why it needs regular practice, but before long you will be considered a good listener. Don't undervalue the non-verbal side. Aspects like eye contact make a huge difference to whether or not you are perceived as listening.

Outcome For both you and those you listen to, good listening skills cut down the stress generated by misunderstanding and poor communication. You will also give the other person the added benefit of feeling valued, building their defence against stress.

Variations None.

Physical control	✪
Emotional/spiritual control	✪✪✪
Defence	✪✪✪✪
Fun	✪✪

5.26 Commuter hell

Preparation None.
Running time 10 minutes.
Resources None.
Frequency Weekly.

If, like me, you work from home, you can ignore this one. But most of us suffer from the irritation of commuting. This is not a matter of road rage (see *Rage*, 5.11 for more on different forms of rage), but a slow build-up of frustration. If you commute an hour each way, you are looking at a 10-hour period each week that has no value in itself. You are also forced to get up earlier than you might want to, and might be missing out in the evening.

Each weekend, put aside a few minutes to plan your commuting. A waste of time? But think how much time you could be making use of. In early sessions you might like to look at alternative timings, routings and transport. If you've been driving to work the same way every day for 10 years, try another route. Mostly, though, think how you can make that wasted time worthwhile. If you're on the train, you can do almost anything. In a car you are more limited, but there's an awful lot that can be done with tapes. Haven't got time to go on a course? Have one in your car. Want to know more about classical music but haven't got the time? You've got plenty.

Feedback The central aim of this approach is to increase the value of the time you spend commuting, making it worthwhile and hence not stressful. However, there's a secondary benefit for those days when you end up in a traffic jam or the trains are running late. By giving commuting intrinsic benefit, you can make it less of a disaster when you spend longer doing it.

Outcome If you are a commuter you owe it to yourself to go beyond the usual paperback novel or the same old radio station. By making something of the journey time you can dramatically reduce its stress-causing properties.

Variations None.

Physical control	✪✪
Emotional/spiritual control	✪✪✪
Defence	✪✪✪
Fun	✪✪✪

5.27 Play!

Preparation None.
Running time 10 minutes.
Resources None.
Frequency Regularly.

Play is a valuable technique that eases stress very naturally. It's sad that we lose a lot of our ability to play as we grow up, when we need it in this respect more than ever. This exercise is not about sport – in fact, most sport isn't play in the sense of being fun and unstructured. Play certainly can be about laughter (see *Laugh!*, 5.7), but here laughter is a secondary component of what is happening.

Find some form of play in which you can totally lose yourself. It might be playing PC games or board games or silly party games. It might be conjuring up a fantasy world on the tube, or trying not to step on the cracks in the pavement, or even saying 'boing' every time you pass someone with red hair. Just play.

Feedback Such play can be undertaken pretty well any time of the day (especially the types than don't involve technology) and can last a few minutes or hours. The great thing about play is not only are you putting aside all your everyday stressors, but the activity you are involved in is deliberately not important. It doesn't matter what happens, it is just play.

Some find it difficult to see how playing a computer game fits with this picture. The right sort of game is an excellent candidate. It has to be something you enjoy and, most importantly, for a single player. Yes, you can get involved, even excited while playing such a game, but underneath you know it does not matter in the slightest. This is why this is a very different technique to sport, which is valuable as physical exercise, but can provide stress of its own because the outcome is more important. Again, multiplayer games are not so effective because other people depend on you and can see how you perform.

Outcome We should all indulge in play more often. It's a great stress reliever.

Variations None.

Physical control	✪✪
Emotional/spiritual control	✪✪✪
Defence	✪✪✪✪
Fun	✪✪✪✪

5.28 Relaxing by numbers

Preparation None.
Running time Five minutes.
Resources A quiet place.
Frequency Occasionally.

If life is getting on top of you, try a little systematic relaxation. It needn't take long, but you do need somewhere quiet to be able to either lie down or sit in a very comfortable chair. Close your eyes, lie back and relax. Try to clear your mind of all thoughts.

Now focus your attention on the parts of your body, working from your head down to your toes. As you consider each section, tense and relax the muscles a few times, holding them tense for a couple of seconds, then relaxing to a long, slow breath. Try to keep your concentration on the area you are exercising – don't let your thoughts drift off to problems or concerns.

When you have worked down the body, lie still, breathe slowly and keep as much as possible to a mind blank of thought for another minute or so. While doing so, keep your muscles as relaxed as possible. When you have finished the exercise, don't jump up, but gently open your eyes and stand slowly.

Feedback Interestingly, a very similar technique is used in the companion book *Instant Brainpower* as a way of improving your visualization skills – an important part of knowledge management. In that case, as you work through your body you are visualizing, but the important component is the parallel feeling of relaxation.

Outcome Although this technique requires a haven from the stressful world, it can be carried out quite quickly, and is a good emergency defence when things are getting on top of you.

Variations You can combine this exercise with a breathing exercise, such as that in 5.17.

Physical control	✪✪✪✪
Emotional/spiritual control	✪✪✪
Defence	✪✪
Fun	✪✪✪

5.29 I agree… ish

Preparation None.
Running time Five minutes.
Resources None.
Frequency Occasionally.

There's no doubt that other people can be particularly stressful. Sometimes a desert island sounds attractive. A particular cause of stress is when someone has something to moan about. It's even worse if they're aggressive, too. You can just feel the stress meter shooting up as they poke their finger towards your nose.

This technique is particularly useful when dealing with such a person. Assuming that you don't want to agree with everything they say and give in entirely (this may be appropriate – if so, go with the flow), find some part of their argument you can agree with and stress your agreement. Don't answer their complaint directly, just confirm how much you agree with them.

For example, say you were dealing with a customer who says she has been a customer for 20 years and is really upset by what has happened, and wants compensation. You have no intention of paying compensation, so help to remove stress from the situation by saying: 'Yes, I can see that this is very upsetting for you, especially when you've been a customer for so long'.

Feedback The technique doesn't just apply to a customer/retailer situation, but anywhere you might have a Mr(s) Angry who wants to complain. It is a special case of *Handling confrontation* (5.2).

Their response may be, 'That's all very well, but what are you going to do about it?', and at that stage to continue saying 'I understand how upsetting this is' will just irritate them. However, in many cases the destressing nature of agreement will be such that you can reach a compromise before the opportunity arises to fight back.

Outcome Reducing the level of anger in a confrontation will increase the chances of reaching an agreement – and will reduce the stress you are being subjected to.

Variations If you don't have someone angry with you right now, congratulations. Try getting a friend to play the part.

Physical control	✪
Emotional/spiritual control	✪✪
Defence	✪✪✪
Fun	✪✪

5.30 You can't take it with you

Preparation None.
Running time 10 minutes.
Resources None.
Frequency Once.

We've identified that stress often arises from a lack of control and self-image. A classic manifestation of this is when your work seeps into your home life. Do you take work home? Do you work on your days off? You need to do something about it. It's both a matter of getting the relaxation and change of focus, and of giving all these excellent stress management techniques a chance.

First, get rid of your briefcase, or at least don't bring it home. If you have to take stuff between home and work (your lunch, say), do it in a clearly non-work-oriented bag or container. Second, examine just why you are bringing material home. It's better to work a little longer, then get home, or better still to get your time better organized so you don't have to work that long. Don't fool yourself that by bringing your work home you are getting a better relationship with your family. It doesn't send the right signals to your children if all you do is to keep telling them to be quiet because you are working, and it will get you even more stressed.

Finally, if there's a special project on that requires you to do some work at weekends (it shouldn't be the norm), go in to work to do it. The atmosphere in out-of-hours workplaces is much more relaxed, and you will have maintained the work/home split.

Feedback This is another example of the benefits of time management to stress management. It isn't enough to not bring work home without doing anything about your time management, as this will just move the stress back to the workplace. See Chapter 6 for the companion *Instant Time Management* and other time management books.

Outcome Protecting your home life from the encroachment of work is a great way to reduce the impact of stress and give you more opportunity to recover.

Variations None.

Physical control	✪✪
Emotional/spiritual control	✪✪✪
Defence	✪✪✪✪
Fun	✪✪

5.31 Café life

Preparation None.
Running time 15 minutes.
Resources None.
Frequency Occasionally.

A favourite quotation of that most philosophical of cartoon characters Wellington in the old *Daily Mirror* Perishers cartoon was 'What is this life if, full of care, we have no time to stand and stare?' This little snippet from the W H Davies poem *Leisure* is not a bad motto for this particular exercise.

Every now and then take yourself off to a café – preferably one with tables on the pavement. Sit down with a cup of your favourite beverage and watch the world go by. Switch off your mobile, don't let your work or home life intrude, just soak up your environment and indulge in some people-watching.

This exercise will not take long, and will amply repay the time, so be prepared to do it during working hours if your boss doesn't mind. If you can take a coffee break away from your desk, do it.

Feedback This technique requires a degree of immediacy. If you have to get in a car and drive to the café, you have reduced the effectiveness. Ideally the location should be within five minutes' walk. If this isn't practical when you are at work, try to fit it in occasionally when you are doing the shopping. If you are lucky enough to work in a building that has built-in pavement coffee bars, so much the better.

To get the value out of this exercise you need to be alone. If you are working near the café (or if it's in your workplace), you may get people joining you to chat – that's fine, don't send them away, but try again another time. Similarly, you really need to do the shopping on your own to get the impact.

Outcome We aren't very good at relaxing, but this is one of the few circumstances when most of us can easily unwind. Try it.

Variations None.

Physical control	✪✪
Emotional/spiritual control	✪✪✪✪
Defence	✪✪✪
Fun	✪✪✪✪

5.32 Get away

Preparation None.
Running time Five minutes.
Resources None.
Frequency Once.

You need to take holidays. Let's say that again in case you missed the point: you need to take holidays. If you usually say with grim delight 'I always carry my leave forward to the next year', you are not helping yourself or the company. It's rare that anyone is so indispensable that an absence of a few days will make a difference.

A good stress-relieving holiday should provide a total change of pace, of inputs (both mental and physical) and of stresses. Avoid holidays that are stressful themselves. If your job involves driving, don't think that a driving tour of the US is the best holiday (though the lack of purpose helps). Ideal stress relief holidays are those where the pace is slowed down. For example, taking a narrowboat along a canal, where you can't go beyond a walking pace, is a great unwinding holiday. Make sure that you have at least a week off – you need that long to really detach yourself. Take a few minutes to think this one through, and schedule a week's break in the next six months. Then stick to it.

Feedback When you go on holiday, don't be tempted to take your mobile phone or your laptop with you. I recently got an e-mail from a colleague who was on holiday with his family. When I suggested he dumped his laptop, he said he was only using it while the rest of his family were reading in the hotel room. That's not good enough. Keep a physical link to the world of work and all the psychological pressures will come pouring through it. Don't do e-mail – read a book or explore or swim.

Outcome A total break is a guaranteed tonic to refresh those batteries. It sometimes feels like the benefits are lost as soon as you get back to work, but in terms of relieving stress you will have worked wonders.

Variations None.

Physical control	✪✪
Emotional/spiritual control	✪✪✪✪
Defence	✪✪✪✪
Fun	✪✪✪✪

5.33 The spiritual path

Preparation None.
Running time 15 minutes.
Resources None.
Frequency Once.

Fifteen minutes is a little quick to achieve spiritual enlightenment, but this exercise is about examining your options. The rest will take longer, quite possibly the rest of your life, but making a start can have an instant impact.

Having a spiritual rock to rely on is very valuable in stress management. It puts the problems causing the stress in context and acts as a source of inner strength. This won't help everyone, but given the statistics showing that most people have some religious belief, however unformed, it may be that you have a resource that you aren't using. Spend a few quiet minutes thinking about what you do believe or would like to know more about. Most religions provide information and courses – consider looking into one or more approaches to spiritual stress management.

Feedback Spiritual matters are difficult to cover in a business book. Apart from anything else, the media convention is to assume that religions are entirely non-factual, while a subject like astrology is given the benefit of the doubt. This contrasts surprisingly with the approach taken by scientists, who pretty well unanimously regard astrology to be without basis, but frequently have a religious belief, or are willing to consider the subject unproved. Until a few years ago, it was often assumed that achieving peace spiritually involved following a far-eastern practice, but the western/middle eastern religions offer better stress management by combining an external focus with equally strong traditions of meditation. If in doubt, the best guidance is probably to start by finding out more about the religion prevalent in your own culture, rather than searching out the exotic.

Outcome No one is going to join a religion just to achieve stress management. However, by giving the spiritual inquisitiveness most of us a feel a chance to get off the rationalist reins for a while, there is an opportunity to explore the stress-relieving benefits of a religious belief.

Variations None.

Physical control	✪
Emotional/spiritual control	✪✪✪✪
Defence	✪✪✪
Fun	✪✪

5.34 Bureaucratic bounce-back

Preparation None.
Running time 10 minutes.
Resources None.
Frequency Occasionally.

Bureaucracy is a regular cause of stress. Almost all bureaucracy started innocently, but the red tape strangles the purpose leaving a stress-inducing tangle. Try a bureaucracy bounce-back session. This can be on your own or in a team meeting. Identify those items of bureaucracy that cause you most stress and see what you can do about it. The action you can take depends on your position in the company and what happens to the output of the bureaucracy. These are the principle options:

- Do nothing – often in bureaucratic systems, nothing is done with the output. What would happen if you simply did nothing?
- Do it your own way – it may be you can fulfil the output requirements of the bureaucracy without going through the required processes.
- Get someone else to do it – this is particularly useful if someone else is trying to impose bureaucracy on you. Push the hassle back onto them.
- Work the system – get the results you want, rather than those the system was designed for.
- Raise awareness at high levels of the system's inadequacy.
- Suggest less bureaucratic alternatives.

Feedback It is possible to do away with bureaucracy on a large scale. See Ricardo Semler's description of this in his book *Maverick!* (see Chapter 6).

Outcome The sheer pointlessness of bureaucracy is depressing and stress-inducing. Bouncing back from bureaucracy is a valuable tool to surviving business stress.

Variations None.

Physical control	✪
Emotional/spiritual control	✪✪
Defence	✪✪✪✪
Fun	✪✪✪

5.35 Because I'm worth it

Preparation None.
Running time Five minutes.
Resources None.
Frequency Once.

Self-esteem is vital in managing stress. Believing that you are worthwhile and giving yourself some time and space counters the hugely stressful position many people find themselves in through lack of control. It's particularly important if you have other people who are strongly dependent on you – children, close family, friends.

Spend five minutes thinking about how your week is divided between doing things for others and doing things that you really want to do. You may find a frightening lack of time for you. Partly this is time management (see Chapter 6 for books to help) – but also it's about valuing yourself. Make sure you get some time in your week that is yours to do with as you wish. This is particularly important if you are self-employed.

Feedback One caveat: the tendency in the latter half of the 20th century was to move increasingly to a self-centred world. People left their families to 'find themselves' or ignored responsibilities in pursuit of pleasure. There is something of a backlash now, because the cost of this cult of the individual has been misery from a breakdown of social values and a realization that the pursuit of success for its own sake isn't particularly rewarding. In looking for stress relief you need to get some space for yourself, but you also need to look outwards as well as inwards. What's needed here, as so often in stress relief, is not placing yourself above everything else, but achieving a balance.

Outcome Finding some time to be you, and to do what you want, is a great opportunity for stress relief. Most of us are out of balance in this respect. But remember the need to look outside yourself as well.

Variations It's easy to put off finding some time for yourself – you are such a busy person, after all. Don't put it off.

Physical control	✪
Emotional/spiritual control	✪✪✪✪
Defence	✪✪✪
Fun	✪✪✪

5.36 E-mail it away

Preparation None.
Running time Two minutes.
Resources E-mail.
Frequency Regularly.

E-mail can be a great tool for stress management. Imagine that you were in the middle of writing an important report. The pressure is on; you have very little time. Suddenly you remember that you haven't organized the materials for tomorrow's meeting. That's important, but you still need to get your report done, so you carry on, while trying to remember to do something about the materials. This exerts stress all along the way – doubly so if you finally forget and don't do anything about it.

One way to relieve that stress is to write yourself a note – but there's still a problem. You have to remember to read the note. Again, there's a nagging memory, continually disrupting your thoughts and adding stress. However, if you've got e-mail always ready to send, in a few seconds you can pull up your e-mail package, write a note to someone to get the job done and send it off. Then you can get back to your report with nothing causing additional stress.

Keep your e-mail running at all times and when such a requirement occurs to you, pop quickly in, send the mail and clear the worry.

Feedback If you want e-mail to alleviate stress rather than cause it, you have to be in control of your e-mail. Many people in corporate environments have e-mail packages set to alert them when mail comes in. This is a recipe for stress, as each arriving mail breaks into your concentration. When you then find out it was junk mail you are doubly stressed by the anticipation and the disappointment.

Some companies still have e-mail systems that can't be activated in a second or two. If yours is one, make a fuss – you need something better.

Outcome It's popular to rubbish e-mail, but used in this way it's a great tool for relieving the stress of sudden thoughts of something that needs doing.

Variations None.

Physical control	✪
Emotional/spiritual control	✪✪
Defence	✪✪✪✪
Fun	✪✪

5.37 Walkies!

Preparation Find location.
Running time 15 minutes.
Resources Suitable footwear.
Frequency Regularly.

Go for a walk. End of technique.

Well, almost. Most physical exercise provides good stress relief, but walking scores highly on a number of counts. It isn't challenging – anyone can do it – it doesn't make you look odd and, unlike most exercise, it isn't mind-numbingly boring.

If possible, walk where you can take in the natural stress relief of the countryside (or at least a park) – fresh air, greenery, lack of traffic. But if you can't get to the countryside, at least get outside and really take in what's around you. Remember to use suitable footwear – trainers might not be your usual style, but they're much better than typical office shoes.

Feedback There are two approaches to stress-relief walking. You can either deliberately keep all your thoughts at bay, or let them work through. In the first approach, focus on your surroundings. Don't let your thoughts wander back to the office. Imagine you were an artist or writer or composer and wanted to capture your surroundings – take them in, both in depth and in overview. If there are people around, take an interest in them (not too obviously) – everyone is interesting.

The alternative approach is to pick whatever's going through your mind most at the moment. The big problem at work or home. Just let the problem and any surrounding facts slosh about in your mind. Don't make a heavy effort to find a solution – let things happen at their own pace.

Outcome Walking gives you the triple benefit of exercise, fresh air and an opportunity for your mind to work in a very different way. As an added bonus, it's a defence against stressors because you're usually out of reach (don't take your mobile). Make it happen.

Variations Fifteen minutes is a sensible minimum that you should be able to do several times a week – half an hour would be even better.

Physical control	✪✪✪✪
Emotional/spiritual control	✪✪✪
Defence	✪✪✪
Fun	✪✪✪

5.38 Sharing chores

Preparation None.
Running time Five minutes.
Resources None.
Frequency Occasionally.

Spend a minute or two thinking through a series of typical days. Look out for regular activities that you don't enjoy, but you always end up doing. These chores could be at home (getting up with the children in the morning, washing up, ironing, putting out the rubbish) or at work (collecting the mail, clearing up, watering the plants).

Look at ways that you can share these tasks around more. Sometimes it will be just a matter of swapping a chore – doing someone else's chores can be surprisingly pleasant compared with doing your own. It may be necessary to renegotiate your division of labour, but if this is the case, go into it positively and lightly. Any attempt to charge in demanding rights is liable to wind everyone up the wrong way.

Feedback The division of a particular chore doesn't have to be equal. It might be that you quite enjoy the job despite its mundane nature, but don't want to do it every time. In such a case, being given a surprise break every few weeks can be just as beneficial as a rota, and much less bureaucratic.

Sometimes, if you are the only one doing a dirty job, it could be because your view of what is important doesn't fit in with everyone else's. If this is the case, try stopping doing it. If you find you can manage without it, fine. If other people miss it, encourage them to join in from now on.

Outcome Chores are small activities that don't seem particularly significant. However, if it's constantly assumed that you will do the dirty jobs, you will find it depressing and stressing. Sharing the chores around makes a lot of difference.

Variations You could use a rota, and sometimes this is inevitable, but try to operate without one first. Few people enjoy the rigidity of a rota – keep it for situations where the task won't get covered otherwise.

Physical control	✪✪
Emotional/spiritual control	✪✪✪
Defence	✪✪✪
Fun	✪✪

5.39 Sleep!

Preparation None.
Running time Five minutes.
Resources None.
Frequency Once.

You only have to speak to someone who has had a baby for the first time to realize how stressful going without sleep can be. We're all conscious of the limited time there is to live a life and want to squeeze every last drop out. That's fine, but insufficient sleep is a sure-fire remedy for stress.

This exercise is to spend a little while thinking about your sleeping pattern and what you can do about it. If you have regular variations in sleep patterns of more than about an hour a day, you are likely to suffer. But it's one thing to prescribe sleep (and only you can determine how much you need), and it's another to get it.

There are mental and physical techniques to help. Make sure you aren't trying to remember something as you go to sleep. If something you need to do next day is nagging at you, jot it down, even if it means getting out of bed. Don't try to go to sleep straight after a passionate discussion – wind down first. If something is going round and round in your head, sit up and pin it down, don't try to force sleep on yourself. When you do lie down, use a calming, tranquil mental image to help you to drift into sleep. Some people find a warm, non-stimulating drink helps. Also a warm bath, followed by getting straight into a warm bed – but make sure the bath isn't hot, as this will stimulate rather than wind down.

Feedback If you are having problems getting to sleep, try relaxation and mental exercises before resorting to drugs. Sleeping pills are rarely an effective answer.

Outcome Sleep deprivation piles stress on stress until you are almost driven mad. If you aim for the sleep you need to feel well, rather than the sleep you can get away with, you are going to underpin all your other efforts in managing stress.

Variations None.

Physical control	✪✪✪✪
Emotional/spiritual control	✪✪✪
Defence	✪✪
Fun	✪✪

5.40 *I did that*

Preparation None.
Running time 10 minutes.
Resources Notepad.
Frequency Once.

As we've seen in various other techniques, there is a strong link between self-esteem and ability to manage stress adequately. This exercise is all about self-esteem.

Sit down with a notepad and note down some of the occasions when you've had a real success in your life. Things that are important to you or things that are important to the world. It could be success in exams and education, getting a job, getting married, having children, the first time you did something successfully that had been hard to achieve (driving a car or beating someone at chess). In one sense these achievements don't have to be large, at least not in the earth-shattering sense, but they need to be significant to you. Little successes are useful too – see *Little successes* (5.1) for more details.

Feedback When you've got together a list of successes – it doesn't matter if it's one or two or a great string – spend some time thinking through what it felt like at the time. Relive the moment when you realized you'd succeeded. Don't feel guilty about enjoying your success; you deserve it. Remembering a moment of success has a surprisingly strong influence on your current feeling of well-being.

Outcome By working on your self-esteem you can add hugely to your ability to stand up to stress and to deflect it. All the evidence is that those with high self-esteem are better able to cope with stress – here's a simple way to reinforce your self-esteem. Don't worry if it sounds artificial, it still works.

Variations You could repeat this exercise, perhaps yearly, looking back over your achievements of the past year.

Physical control	✪
Emotional/spiritual control	✪✪✪✪
Defence	✪
Fun	✪✪✪

5.41 Broken record

Preparation Invent scenario.
Running time Five minutes.
Resources A stooge.
Frequency Once.

We've all been there. You know you're right, but the person you are talking to just won't give in. You can almost feel the steam coming out from under your collar. Imagine a situation in which you have to complain about something. Persuade a colleague to act as a stooge in trying out this scenario. His or her role is to counter your request. For example, you could be taking back a broken product and demanding a replacement, or asking for a refund in a restaurant. Use the traditional assertion technique of 'broken record'. Simply repeat your request whatever the stooge says. Don't go on too long, but do go on significantly longer than the comfort factor will allow.

Feedback This technique is slightly risky, as there is the possibility of making the other person angry, and hence generating rather than reducing stress. Make sure that you keep your repeated request for the information low key and friendly. Nod, agree, say 'Yes, I see,' to the other person's reasons for not coming up with the goods – then ask again. This technique is best used face to face; it is too easy for the other person to just put the phone down. If you find it very difficult, practise some more – it becomes relatively easy and can even be enjoyable.

Outcome It is surprising how often this technique will whittle away resistance and get a result. It's not one you want to use too often, or somewhere where you are a regular visitor, but it can sometimes be very effective.

Variations If there is a genuine reason to practise the technique, so much the better. This could either be in the sort of scenario used here (complaint) or when you are trying to get information from a reluctant source. A close variant is to keep up the same request, but phrase it differently each time.

Physical control	✪
Emotional/spiritual control	✪✪
Defence	✪✪✪✪
Fun	✪✪

5.42 Coherent discussion

Preparation None.
Running time Five minutes.
Resources None.
Frequency Regularly.

Traditional discussion is like the output of a light bulb – rays head off in all sorts of directions with no focus or unanimity. By contrast, the rays of a laser's coherent light are in step and the result is a much more powerful beam. Similarly, a coherent discussion will generate less stress and produce better output.

Before running a meeting, consider how to structure the discussion. Separate off different approaches so that you are all working together, rather than fighting each other. A meeting structure might be something like:

- Review what the meeting intends to achieve.
- Brainstorm (or use other creativity techniques to generate) some new ideas.
- Select the most appealing idea on gut feel.
- Get feedback on the group's feelings.
- Spend a few minutes improving the good points.
- Spend a few minutes fixing any negative points.
- Devise a handful of milestones and timescales for action.

Feedback The structure used is up to the group. The importance is in getting people working coherently rather than destructively. When engaged in one activity, try to keep off the others. When coming up with ideas don't criticize, and when assessing good points, don't let any 'buts' creep in.

Outcome Much of the stress from bad meetings comes out of badly managed discussion. Coherence helps everyone.

Variations See Edward de Bono's *Six Thinking Hats* (Chapter 6).

Physical control	✪
Emotional/spiritual control	✪✪✪
Defence	✪✪✪✪
Fun	✪✪

5.43 Music soothes the savage breast

Preparation Get appropriate CDs or tapes.
Running time Five minutes.
Resources Tape or CD-player.
Frequency Regularly.

Often stress strikes at a time when we can't do anything about it. One of the reasons road rage is so common and extreme is that you are highly restrained by the physical and mental requirements of driving a car. You can't start exercising or have a massage – but you can use music. The right sort of music will lower your heart rate, get you thinking in a more relaxed way and generally put your stress into perspective.

Note 'the right sort of music'. Not all music is destressing. Anything with a fast beat and a heavy, pulsing bass will act more as an adrenalin booster than a relaxant. And don't think just because it's classical it's calming – there's plenty of classical music that will push up your heart rate.

Look for slow, calm music, reminiscent of flowing water and happy, untroubled times. It can be anything from classical to folk as long as it has the right effect. I find Tudor and Elizabethan church music, which combines a steady, flowing quality with spiritual depth, particularly effective. The best idea is to try a few different styles and see which suits you best. See Chapter 6 for some more specific suggestions.

Feedback Make sure that the music that is relieving your stress isn't stressing others. The tinny rattle of overheard Walkman headphones or the booming bass of a car passing with its stereo up too loud causes plenty of irritation for others. Try to keep your music to yourself.

Outcome With appropriate music you can distance yourself from stress and put it into perspective. It slows down your heart rate and even helps regular breathing. There's nothing better if you are stuck in a traffic jam.

Variations Music isn't just valuable in the car. The right kind of music can be an aid to relaxation and stress relief wherever you are.

Physical control	✪
Emotional/spiritual control	✪✪✪✪
Defence	✪
Fun	✪✪✪✪

5.44 Fall-out shelters

Preparation None.
Running time 10 minutes.
Resources Notebook.
Frequency Once.

Since the ability to deal with stress is strongly connected with control and self-image, it is well worth constructing a stress fall-out shelter, particularly at work. Spend around five minutes thinking about the personal elements of life that help you to deal with stress. Imagine that you were building yourself a stress-proof bunker. What would you incorporate? It might involve quite mundane items. Typical contents might be:

- family photographs;
- a print of your favourite painting;
- photographs of restful scenes;
- a pair of slippers;
- a comfy chair;
- a sound system.

... but it might involve something more bizarre.

Now spend the rest of the exercise getting together a list of small actions that would be needed to move your current position into something closer to your bunker. Make sure that some of these actions are carried out in the first week.

Feedback The image of a bunker or shelter might be misleading. You aren't trying to cut yourself off from the world or all its influences. It is stress and its fall-out that you are sheltering from.

Outcome The stress shelter isn't going to keep all stress away from you, but it will boost your stress management in an unspectacular but effective manner.

Variations Although this exercise is primarily aimed at the workplace, you may well find that something similar is necessary in the home. Having somewhere quiet to retire to for five minutes, whether it's a study or a garden shed, can help a lot.

Physical control	✪✪
Emotional/spiritual control	✪✪✪✪
Defence	✪✪✪
Fun	✪✪✪

5.45 Pet solution

Preparation Obtain pet.
Running time Five minutes.
Resources Pet.
Frequency Regularly.

There is ample evidence that pets reduce stress levels and anxiety. This is now recognized to the extent that pets are allowed into some hospitals to help with the recovery of patients. You will need to obtain a pet – the instant part comes later. Take some time to think about the lifetime of the pet. You may be taking on a commitment that runs into decades. Consider how much maintenance is required. Is no one at home all day? Are you away a lot? How would you cope? The actual technique, once you've got the pet, is to spend some quality time with it. Stroke the pet if feasible. Even stroking while watching TV can help, but for maximum destressing benefit, give it some time on its own. The sessions needn't be long to be noticeably beneficial.

Feedback There is a rough spectrum of pets: the higher up the scale the greater the commitment, but (usually) the greater the return. A few key points on it:

- Goldfish – very low commitment. Grow much bigger and last much longer in a pond; watching them in the pond is more therapeutic than a tank (though weather dependent).
- Hamster – only lives around two years, but can be stroked. Very variable in personality. Sleeps a lot in the day.
- Rat/guinea pig/rabbit – longer life, more commitment. Select rat for intelligence, guinea pig for docile stroking and rabbit... if you like rabbits.
- Cat – looks after itself a fair amount of the day. Less docile than a guinea pig and not as friendly as a dog, but plenty of personality.
- Dog – the ultimate stress-relieving pet, but also by far the most commitment.

Outcome Having a pet about the place is both a source of calming interaction and a non-threatening interest. Give it serious consideration.

Variations If owning a pet isn't practical, see if you can gain regular access to someone else's pet.

Physical control	✪✪✪
Emotional/spiritual control	✪✪✪
Defence	✪
Fun	✪✪✪✪

5.46 Life, the universe and everything

Preparation None
Running time 10 minutes.
Resources None.
Frequency Occasionally.

One of the main motivations for exploring the spiritual dimension is the realization that money and property aren't everything. Of course, we all want to be comfortable, and many people would like to be rich, but the consistent story from those who have it all in material terms is that it isn't enough.

Spend a few minutes thinking about the end of your life. This isn't morbid, it's something we know is going to happen. What would you like to look back over and feel happy about? There will probably be elements of money and possessions, but get a full picture. Try to get a feel for the balance.

With this picture in mind, look at your activities. Could you include more that doesn't involve wealth and possessions? Can you achieve a better balance, and hence reduce the feeling that something is missing from your life? In the few minutes available, try to come up with a couple of possible directions that you can work on over the next few months.

Feedback Some miss out by pursuing the material at the expense of everything else. The people who miss out on family life to concentrate on their career. The people for whom accumulating more and more money is the only driver. The people who think having fun (or lunch) is for wimps – they just don't have time for it. This exercise is about you – the very core of what you are and the reasons behind it. Don't skip over it if you think it sounds too wishy-washy, it is entirely concrete.

Outcome Particularly as you reach mid-life, the discomfort that all your achievements are centred around earning money and accumulating possessions can become a heavy burden. Aiming for a more balanced life is going to help to iron out these stresses.

Variations This is one that's worth coming back to now and again to see how you are doing.

Physical control	✪
Emotional/spiritual control	✪✪✪✪
Defence	✪✪✪✪
Fun	✪✪

5.47 Nemesis

Preparation None
Running time 10 minutes.
Resources None.
Frequency Once.

This technique is only relevant if there's someone you have regular contact with who is a major stressor in his or her own right. Spend a few minutes thinking about the people you deal with. Is there someone who has a physical effect on your well-being? After being with them, do you feel ill, are you dizzy, does your head or heart pound? How about damp palms or a dry mouth? If there isn't, fine. If there is, you need to do something. Consider these two major options.

In a surprising number of work cases, the answer can be to terminate the relationship. Actively avoid them. Keep out of their way. Avoid stress. If necessary, make changes to one of your jobs to make this more likely. But this isn't always the answer, especially where the person might be part of your family. If you decide that the answer is to stay in the relationship, though, you can't leave things as they are. Try to stand back and observe a confrontation. What is it about the other person that causes the reaction in you? Try to understand it, and look for ways of circumventing it.

Only you can observe your feelings, but it would help, if there's someone you really trust, to get someone else's views on what is happening, too.

Feedback It is tempting to think that we should be able to brush over any personal difficulties because we're 'professional people' or because personalities aren't important in business. In fact, personal aspects have much more influence than we admit. If there is a major clash that is stressing you, action is necessary.

Outcome If you are in regular contact with someone who causes you stress just through that contact, it is essential you do something about it, whether it is to sever the contact or to deflect the stress. Otherwise it can be a dangerously persistent stressor.

Variations None.

Physical control	✪✪
Emotional/spiritual control	✪✪✪
Defence	✪✪✪✪
Fun	✪

5.48 Natural release

Preparation None
Running time 30 minutes.
Resources Exercise environment.
Frequency Regularly.

Regular exercise (see *Stress workout*, 5.5) is a valuable part of stress management, but you can go one step further. Pushing yourself to the limit in the gym may have great aerobic benefits, but it is about as inspiring as working on a production line – in fact, it is the production line approach to exercise, and as such the least effective at stress management.

Investigate ways of exercising where you can also benefit from the natural stress relief of fresh air and beautiful scenery. Don't jog on a treadmill, go for a run in a park or even better in the country. Don't use a rowing machine, find somewhere where you can row on a river or lake. Take up rural bike rides. Or try taking vigorous walks in pleasant surroundings (see *Walkies!*, 5.37). Spend a few minutes thinking how you can give your exercise routine a natural boost.

Feedback The stress control factors here are surprisingly complex. It isn't just the physical benefit of clean air. The colours and lines of the countryside seem to have a natural ability to remove stress. Just standing at a viewpoint, watching the evening sunlight change across fields and hills gives a wonderful sense of serenity. Add to this the other sensory inputs, and you are providing much more than you might imagine.

We can't all just walk out of our door into the countryside, and even if we can, a whole combination of weather and darkness may conspire against it being practical every time. This doesn't mean that it can't work for you. You might not be able (or want) to make your entire exercise routine in a natural environment, but make sure that you make regular excursions to give a natural flavour. Plan the first one, now.

Outcome By combining exercise with a satisfying natural environment you can attack stress on both physical and spiritual fronts simultaneously.

Variations None.

Physical control	✪✪✪✪
Emotional/spiritual control	✪✪✪
Defence	✪
Fun	✪✪✪

5.49 Information overload

Preparation None
Running time 10 minutes.
Resources None.
Frequency Once.

It's a fact of modern life – information is pervasive. This is a good thing. The Internet for example is an amazing information resource, on your desktop 24 hours a day. Yet it can all get too much. There are all those reports and files and newspapers and correspondence... and, and, and it goes on. Having all this information dumped on you can result in significant stress. But it doesn't have to be like that. Spend a few minutes putting together a personal strategy for managing overload.

- Quick-sort your mail – dump junk and scan-read possible junk.
- Manage e-mail – only look at it a few times a day and clear your in-box daily. Use filters to remove obvious rubbish.
- Cut down on newspapers and magazines (see *No news is good news*, 5.53).
- Return all reports more than one page long unread with a notation to this effect.

Use the 80:20 rule (see *Pareto*, 5.59). Usually 20 per cent of your documents carry 80 per cent of the value. Be ruthless. Try to move from a push approach to information to a pull approach. Simply cutting out all input leaves you without the information you actually need. Balance the reduction in incoming data with knowledge on how to find the information you need when you want it.

Feedback Strangely, one outcome of managing information overload is that you can read more. Most of us don't read enough fiction or general non-fiction. By vastly cutting down on the unnecessary words you read, you can up the quantity of more enjoyable input (this includes business books – if they're boring, dump them).

Outcome The fact that there's so much information out there is a joy if you exert control over how and when you receive it. This exercise is about regaining that control, an essential for stress management.

Variations None.

Physical control	✪
Emotional/spiritual control	✪✪
Defence	✪✪✪✪
Fun	✪✪✪

5.50 Honesty

Preparation None
Running time Two minutes.
Resources None.
Frequency Occasionally.

Every now and then we get the opportunity to cut off a stressor before it can produce problems. Conscious dishonesty can prey on your mind and become a chronic source of stress. The impact isn't the same for everyone. For some, receiving stolen goods is no problem, while for others accepting 10p too much in their change at the supermarket can be as insistent a worry as toothache.

Before you take a consciously dishonest action, however trivial, pause for a moment. Consider taking the honest path – it can lead to some surprising benefits when others compliment you on your honesty, and it will certainly reduce stress levels.

Feedback Don't confuse honesty with misguided bluffness. 'I speak as I find' is at best an excuse. Saying what you think, whatever it is, and being 'totally honest' in this sense is not positive stress management, in fact it is a major source of stress, particularly for others.

Honesty is not a particularly popular virtue in present-day culture. While social and environmental consciences are on the increase, there are many aspects of honesty that aren't considered important by many. To make this technique of value you need to have an honest(!) assessment of your own limits.

Outcome By avoiding acts of dishonesty that your own conscience will nag you for, you can remove this area of self-generated stress.

Variations None.

Physical control	✪
Emotional/spiritual control	✪✪
Defence	✪✪✪
Fun	✪✪

5.51 Different values

Preparation None
Running time Five minutes.
Resources None.
Frequency Once.

This is a thought exercise. First consider this research. A 1999 edition of *Demography Magazine* carried a study based on survey data from 1987 on 28,000 individuals. Around 2,000 of these people had died between the survey being taken and the 1999 study. In general terms, it turned out that people who attended religious services of any kind at least once a week lived, on average, seven years longer. The comment of someone involved in the study was: 'People who attend church have friends to count on and a sense of their importance in the scheme of things.'

This exercise is not about attending religious services, but about considering how the difference in approach to life and personal values seems to have influenced the stress levels of those concerned. Spend a few minutes thinking about how you use your life. Are there opportunities to take a step back from frantic pursuits? It might be worth finding something that is your equivalent of being part of a religious group.

Feedback There is a always a danger in statistics of confusing correlation and causality. Two facts can have a matching pattern (correlation) without any direct link between them. For example, for a number of years after the Second World War, there was a strong correlation between banana imports and pregnancies, but no one suggests that bananas caused the pregnancy. Similarly, it is possible that there isn't a causal link between attending regular religious services and an extended lifespan. However, it seems likely that a combination of a local support network and the opportunity to step back from stress were major contributory factors.

Outcome There may be no outcome at all, but giving some consideration to the benefits of finding a support network and a way to put your life into context is worth the investment of a few minutes.

Variations None.

Physical control	✪
Emotional/spiritual control	✪✪✪✪
Defence	✪✪
Fun	✪✪

5.52 Stimulants stink

Preparation None
Running time Five minutes.
Resources None.
Frequency Once.

At least, stimulants stink from the stress-relief viewpoint. They are sometimes valuable and often enjoyable. This exercise isn't an attempt to get you to give up stimulants, just to raise awareness of the stimulants in regular use so that you can cut them down when under pressure. Anything with significant caffeine content is an obvious contender (coffee, tea, chocolate products, colas). If you are feeling stressed, cut down your consumption. Particularly avoid them before going to bed or you can have a double dose of stress from sleep disruption.

Other less obvious stimulants are alcohol and smoking, both often considered calming. Unfortunately, alcohol is a stimulant, and the effect of excessive alcohol can be to encourage actions that will cause more stress when the drink has worn off. Similarly, nicotine pumps up the heart rate, not something you want when you are trying to be calm.

Feedback Try a few of the caffeine-free alternatives. Most people, for instance, who 'need' a cup of coffee to get going in the morning find that decaffeinated coffee is just as effective. These days, herb teas are much more pleasant than they used to be – consider them if you are a tea drinker. Many people who have removed caffeine entirely from their diet say that it has a very positive effect on their general feeling of well-being. Giving up smoking is a no-brain decision (though certainly not easy), but moderate alcohol use is much less clear-cut. With some evidence that a regular glass of red wine is beneficial for the heart, and general appreciation of the benefits of controlled use of alcohol, it's hard to argue against it entirely – but consideration of amounts and timing makes a lot of sense.

Outcome A reduction in consumption of everyday stimulants will help you to keep calm and to wind down at the end of the day. Most of us could moderate our habitual stimulant consumption to some degree.

Variations None.

Physical control	✪✪✪✪
Emotional/spiritual control	✪✪
Defence	✪
Fun	✪✪

5.53 No news is good news

Preparation None
Running time 10 minutes.
Resources None.
Frequency Once.

A constant diet of depressing news is stressful. We like balance, but rarely get it. In the 1990s, a BBC newscaster made the controversial statement that there isn't enough good news – that reporters and editors don't balance the news content. It didn't help his career, but it's true. Spend a few minutes assessing your weekly news input. Consider all media. Now try to break it into rough categories, like business, home news, foreign news, sport, etc. For each, get a feel for the media you use, and the value it has to your work and social life.

Finally, consider a few experiments to get a better fit with your personal requirements. Your needs will vary, but here are a few possible approaches:

- Cancel your daily newspaper. Only buy a paper when you have leisure time and want to do something different. If you read it when commuting, read a range of books instead.
- Don't watch more than one TV bulletin a day. Shop around to find the one that best suits you on content and approach, rather than your habitual one.
- Have at least one day a week when you don't take in any news other than by word of mouth.
- Replace other forms of news with an Internet news summary.
- Have several longer news holidays (a week to a month) during the year.

Feedback An immediate response is that 'I can't possibly do that'. In fact it's amazing how little news you really need, and most of that is either business or leisure specific. For the rest, select what you enjoy, not what is expected.

Outcome One reason that news can be particularly stressful is that you are being given lots of danger signals with no possibility for action. By reducing the constant flow of news you can reduce this impact. As a bonus, you will free up wasted time, too.

Variations None.

Physical control	✪
Emotional/spiritual control	✪✪✪
Defence	✪✪✪✪
Fun	✪✪✪

5.54 The timescales game

Preparation None
Running time Two minutes.
Resources None.
Frequency Regularly.

Often stress is generated unnecessarily because we get a problem or a task out of all proportion. A handy way to put a problem in its place is to think about time. You'll find a number of exercises in this book that are about time management. This is more about understanding time and its impact.

Next time you've got a problem or task that is nagging at you or causing stress, take a couple of minutes to think about two aspects of time. Is this really a problem now, or are you anticipating something well into the future? When does the task actually need to be completed by? Second, think yourself well into the future. Looking back from 10 years away, how significant would this problem or task be? How much difference is it going to make to the rest of your life?

Feedback Sometimes the answer will be 'It needs doing today' or 'It's going to change the rest of my life'. Fine – this may well be a circumstance where a little stress is desirable. If, however, it's one of the many, many problems and tasks that aren't urgent, or that you wouldn't even be able to remember existed in 10 years' time however it turned out, it's time to loosen up.

Outcome Giving a time context to a problem or task, and looking back on it from an imaginary future is a valuable approach to remove plenty of unnecessary stress.

Variations This is an exercise that you can do whenever a problem or task gets on top of you.

Physical control	✪
Emotional/spiritual control	✪✪✪
Defence	✪✪✪✪
Fun	✪✪

5.55 Setbacks

Preparation None
Running time Five minutes.
Resources None.
Frequency Regularly.

Sometimes an apparently trivial setback can really hurt. Like most writers, I have a thick pile of rejection letters. Having a book rejected seems pretty low in the scheme of things, but when it's an idea you poured your heart into, rejection is very painful. The same goes for any setback. To make matters worse, failures sometimes come in clumps. It's not fate or being jinxed – if you think about it, a series of problems wouldn't be random if they were all nicely spread out. By the time you've hit your third setback in a row you can be feeling very low and very stressed.

The technique here is ancient, but it still works. If a child is learning to ride a bike, we encourage it to get straight back on after a fall. Similarly, when hit by a setback, launch another initiative as soon as possible. This could involve a small change, be loosely related or be totally different. So, for instance, when I get a rejection on a book I might send the same proposal to a different publisher, or rework the proposal, or send out a totally different proposal addressing a different market. If you get a real downer, you can increase the reinforcement by doubling the response. If a rejection really upsets me, I send out not one proposal but two.

Feedback Timing is important. React quickly, ideally within a few hours. The knowledge of impending action will cut out a lot of the impact straight away.This technique demonstrates the power of anticipation. Anticipation is often better than reality. If you can set up a positive anticipation of something that equals or betters the setback, you can largely counter its impact.

Outcome Some setbacks are so big that nothing will counter them effectively. But for the vast majority, this technique will push you back into a positive frame of mind, not giving stress a chance to take a hold.

Variations None.

Physical control	✪
Emotional/spiritual control	✪✪✪
Defence	✪✪✪✪
Fun	✪✪

5.56 Boomerang compliments

Preparation None
Running time Two minutes.
Resources None.
Frequency Regularly.

This is the complement to *Don't do that* (5.21). There we look at the impact of being negative. Here we are considering the reinforcing nature of being positive in an active way. It shouldn't be too much of a surprise, but when you are nicer to other people, on the whole, they are nicer to you. Smile at them and they will smile at you. Say nice things to them and they'll say nice things back.

Before long it will become natural, but to start with you may need to take a slightly artificial approach to this. Not artificial pleasantness, but artificial action. Try to thank somebody for something every day – unless you spend your day locked in a room you will find there is something worth thanking someone for. Associate smiling with walking. When you encounter people you are often on your feet – help those smiles to become natural.

Feedback This is not asking you to be toadying or overly nice. Most people are very sensitive to falseness and it will result in raised hackles. Instead, I am advocating genuine pleasantness. Not an artificial, robotic smile, but a genuine look of pleasure at seeing someone. Of course, you don't like everyone – this is inevitable – but most people find most others quite pleasant enough to be nice to them. Give it a try.

Outcome The very action of being pleasant and smiling will help to relax you and drain tension. But the result will be felt twice over, as pleasantness, like a boomerang, tends to come back to the originator. Other people will be nicer, and that, too, will lower your stress level.

Variations None.

Physical control	✪✪✪
Emotional/spiritual control	✪✪✪
Defence	✪✪✪✪
Fun	✪✪✪

5.57 Children

Preparation Have children.
Running time Two minutes.
Resources None.
Frequency Regularly.

If you haven't got children, don't feel you have to rush out and get some just to do this exercise. If you do have them, though, whatever age they are, they are a very ambiguous influence on stress. There are times when they make you feel wonderful… and times when they make life hell.

When your children cause stress (when, not if), find a way to take a step back from the situation for a couple of minutes. Put the stress in context. Divert your feeling from anger into compassion or amusement. Often a stressful situation with a child develops as you begin to react negatively – if you can catch the anger and substitute amusement you are well on the way to overcoming the stress.

It is often easier to describe this process than to do it. If it proves a problem, look for outside sources of stress. For example, is your stress when your children play around instead of getting ready for school caused by the child or by the need to get to school on time? Put the requirement in proportion and act accordingly. 'Your children don't want your attention for long, before long you'll be asking them for attention' might be a cliché, but it's true. Look for ways to enjoy the experience instead of suffering.

Feedback One problem with dealing with this stress issue is that it isn't politically correct to admit that having children can be hell. Parenting is supposed to be a 'warm, sharing experience' and books on childcare are full of the virtues of being reasonable. Tell that to the average five-year-old (or even worse, your five-year-old).

Outcome The stress caused by children is chronic, and as such more dangerous in the long-term than one-off big stresses. Working on it can bring you a lot of advantages, and may also help your relationship with your child.

Variations Look into alternative approaches in childcare manuals.

Physical control	✪✪
Emotional/spiritual control	✪✪✪✪
Defence	✪✪✪
Fun	✪✪

5.58 Meditation

Preparation None
Running time 10 minutes.
Resources Quiet space.
Frequency Regularly.

For some, meditation is a natural part of life, for others a symptom of the lunatic fringe. In fact, there is nothing extreme about meditation, nor does it require acceptance of a particular philosophy. Find somewhere you can sit quietly and comfortably – unless you are very supple, cross-legged positions should be avoided. Reduce sensory distractions to a minimum. Breathe slowly and evenly. Imagine that everything is slowing down.

Then, find a focus. This can be a meaningless set of syllables, a simple phrase, or a very calm image like a great, unruffled lake, or a single leaf. To begin with, you may find it helps to have a physical object to provide the focus, but before long you will be able to do without it. If you use an object, don't think about any associations or properties it has. Keep your focus on the entire object. For a few minutes (with your eyes closed unless you are using something physical), let your focus fill your mind. The stress will drain away – but don't think about it, or its causes.

Feedback Initially you will find it hard to keep focused. Your mind will wander. When you notice this, bring yourself back. Don't go too long to start with. Begin with a few minutes and build up to maybe 15 minutes.

Most of the world's religions, from Christianity to Zen Buddhism and plenty of non-religious groups, practise meditation. You can see it as an opportunity to explore inner spirituality or as a simple mental/physical exercise. One effect is to change the brainwave pattern to a less reactive one (see Chapter 1). Whatever your view, it works.

Outcome Meditation is hard to do without a quiet space and a few undisturbed minutes, but its powerful impact on stress levels makes it well worth trying.

Variations Try using a kitchen timer to avoid worrying about how long you have been meditating, particularly if you have another activity to undertake later.

Physical control	✪✪✪
Emotional/spiritual control	✪✪✪✪
Defence	✪
Fun	✪✪✪

5.59 Pareto

Preparation None.
Running time Five minutes.
Resources None.
Frequency Once.

The 19th-century Italian economist Vilfredo Pareto discovered that 80 per cent of the wealth was owned by 20 per cent of the people. Since then, the 80:20 rule has been found to apply in many circumstances. The 80:20 rule is at the core of time management (see Chapter 6 for more on time management). Once you recognize that you can achieve 80 per cent completion with 20 per cent of the effort, time management becomes a lot more practical – and so does stress management, because losing control of your time inevitably leads to stress.

Think about that huge 80 per cent that the final polishing takes. Sometimes that remainder is vital. You don't want a nuclear power plant that's 80 per cent safe. However, for most tasks (could it be 80 per cent of them?), 80 per cent success is fine. When you are setting goals and milestones, wherever possible use an 80:20 target. That way, you are much less likely to get into that gut-wrenching state where you've never time to get anything done.

Feedback For some of us, Pareto is absolutely natural. We are happy with approximate solutions that do the job. For others it is a real wrench – a 'botched job'. This technique is not an excuse for sloppiness, but a plea for accepting a very good result rather than striving for perfection. Would this preclude the great works of art, the great theories of science ever being developed? Maybe, but lots of great thinkers and artists work very quickly – greatness isn't always about nit-picking.

Outcome The potential for freeing up time is enormous. If you moved everything from perfectionism to Pareto you would free up 80 per cent of your time. That won't happen, but the time you can release will give you a buffer against stress.

Variations Consider other aspects of time management (see Chapter 6 for time management books) when looking at stress management – time management isn't just for anal retentives, it really helps.

Physical control	✪✪✪
Emotional/spiritual control	✪
Defence	✪✪✪
Fun	✪✪

5.60 Bully off

Preparation None.
Running time One week.
Resources None.
Frequency Once.

We are all familiar with the classroom advice: 'You should stand up to bullies, they are cowards, really.' And perhaps we also remember the way that this advice seemed dubious when the bully responded by wittily punching us on the nose. Bullying doesn't stop at school. It is common in the workplace (and out of it). The difference is that threats and abused power usually replace violence.

It should be easier to face up to a bully as an adult, but the social pressure not to is often strong; even so, the advice stands. In some circumstances, it will be enough to point out that it isn't polite or acceptable to act or speak a certain way. If this doesn't work, calmly threaten to use whatever channels are available to get something done about it. If there is still no change, resort to formal means – it might seem overkill for bullying, but this practice can keep the bullied person in continuous stress.

For this exercise, spend a week consciously looking out for bullying in the workplace. Watch how you and others act. Observe how you are treated and how others are treated. Take action if necessary.

Feedback Perhaps you are fortunate and there is no bullying in your working environment, but even if you are lucky, it will have been worth undertaking the exercise. It should not take up much time, hence it's still reasonably instant, despite taking a week.

Outcome An awareness of bullying and the basic steps you can take to do something about it can help to relieve your own stress and that of your colleagues.

Variations If you are involved on either end of the bullying and can't take an objective view it might be worth bringing in an external person to untangle things, but you are the only one who can assert yourself against a bully – someone else can't do it for you.

Physical control	✪
Emotional/spiritual control	✪✪
Defence	✪✪✪✪
Fun	✪

5.61 Pampering

Preparation As appropriate.
Running time 15 minutes.
Resources Budget.
Frequency Occasionally.

When everything is getting on top of you, indulge in a little pampering. Don't listen to excuses about not having the time, or not being able to afford it. If it works, it's worth blowing some of your budget (personal or business) on the exercise. Exactly what pampering is differs hugely from individual to individual. Find something you really enjoy that will take you out of yourself and get you going. Don't make excuses, make it happen within a few days of feeling that everything's miserable.

Feedback A problem with pampering is the media image. TV and movies usually simplify a concept by introducing an archetypal version. After a while, such is the strength of the media that we confuse the archetype with reality. Thanks to TV and movies, pampering conjures up images of extreme luxury, five-star hotels, massage and beauty treatment, haute cuisine, waiters and flunkies.

This image of pampering is fine if you are comfortable with these trappings. On TV recently a young couple were sent to an exclusive hotel in a romantic location. They felt cowed by the formal environment and caused themselves significant embarrassment and stress until they got moved to a more down-market hotel. Make sure that pampering is within your comfort zone; don't try to match some glossy image. It may be that your idea of being pampered is having a curry delivered and eating it in front of the TV. If so, this will relax you more than a six-course meal at a country house hotel. I'm not saying it's bad to expand your horizons, but when looking to be pampered go for an environment and experience that won't cause you stress.

Outcome Properly managed, pampering is a great way to unwind and destress. It's important, though, that this exercise is occasional. While a weekly event can be a useful ritual (see *Ritual relaxation*, 5.13), pampering has to be more irregular to have impact.

Variations None.

Physical control	✪✪✪
Emotional/spiritual control	✪✪✪✪
Defence	✪✪
Fun	✪✪✪✪

5.64 Going solo

Preparation Plan location.
Running time Half day.
Resources Transport.
Frequency Occasionally.

We are sometimes so obsessed with socialization – being together with our friends, family, spouse, children – that we forget the benefits of a little time alone. Take half a day to have some time totally on your own. Do what you find relaxing. It might be walking in the country or taking in architecture. It might be serious shopping or just sitting somewhere peaceful with a good book. The most important thing is to be alone.

Feedback If half a day doesn't seem exactly instant, bear in mind that there doesn't have to be lots of planning involved.

This technique is only effective for stress relief if you don't feel guilty about doing it. After all, it seems somehow treacherous to admit that getting away from your family or friends can be good for you or enjoyable. The implication seems to be that you don't like to be with them. Yet everyone sometimes needs a little space to be alone, and often the pressures of work and family life leave little time unless you make it. Don't feel guilty.

Sometimes the hardest part is describing this need to those who are close to you and might dislike the thought that you want to be away from them. Explaining how you need 'space' may be considered pretentious. It could be easier simply to arrange circumstances so it happens this way, rather than trying to justify it. This isn't a matter of lying or being devious – just fit it in with some other activity that the others want to do but you don't.

Outcome By being alone for a little while you can sometimes achieve a peace that is difficult to achieve under normal circumstances.

Variations None.

Physical control	✪✪
Emotional/spiritual control	✪✪✪
Defence	✪
Fun	✪✪✪

5.65 Doing drugs

Preparation None.
Running time 10 minutes.
Resources None.
Frequency Once.

This is more of an information section than a true exercise. Most people can manage stress without the use of drugs – it is pretty obvious that, if you can, you should. Sometimes a doctor will prescribe drugs to help with stress. If you are prescribed drugs, or are thinking of asking for them, here are a few thoughts:

- Sleeping pills – a common cause of stress is not sleeping well. Before resorting to sleeping pills, check out our suggestions on sleep (5.39) and aromatherapy (5.12). It is also worth looking at the various other recommendations throughout the book on relaxation and switching off. Sleeping pills don't really deliver a good night's sleep, rapidly become ineffective and can be addictive.
- Tranquillizers – traditional tranquillizers are addictive, and are only usually prescribed for specific, major conditions. The alternative, beta-blockers, are more widely used to cope with a one-off trauma as they are effective and non-addictive. Be aware, though, that they do have a number of potential side effects.
- Anti-depressants – depression is a specific medical condition, rather than simply feeling sad. Modern drugs can be very effective, although they do take days or weeks before they have an effect. Most have side effects, which sometimes are considered worse than the original problem, but for some individuals anti-depressants will prove very effective.

Feedback The essential thing when considering the use of drugs in stress relief is that it is with the active involvement of a medical professional – these are not drugs for self-administration. For most people, good stress management without the use of drugs will be sufficient – but consult your doctor if in any doubt.

Outcome The outcome of this exercise is to put the use of drugs into context.

Variations None.

Physical control	✪✪✪✪
Emotional/spiritual control	✪
Defence	✪
Fun	✪

5.66 Phone control

Preparation None.
Running time Five minutes.
Resources None.
Frequency Once.

Phones are superb stress generators. They have no respect for your time or timings – they ring as and when they like. Use an answering machine, voicemail or someone else answering your phone to protect times when you need to be undisturbed. At such times, switch off the phone or get away from it, so you aren't aware of the incoming calls, otherwise you will keep wondering who it was and what they wanted.

Key times to protect are important social events, meals and thinking time. Beware, however, of becoming the sort of person who always hides behind someone else or the voicemail. You will get a reputation for being a slacker or someone who doesn't care. Make sure there are substantial times of the day when you do answer your phone yourself.

If you receive messages, make sure you ring back during the next 24 hours or working day (unless there are exceptional circumstances). If there is one thing worse than someone who always hides behind voicemail, it's someone who hides behind voicemail then never replies.

Feedback Answering machines and voicemail are the standard remedies for phone stress, but be aware of one perverse counter-reaction. If you are waiting for a call that is important to you, and you need to talk to someone immediately, there is nothing worse than going out of the room for five minutes, only to find a voicemail message from that person – and you can never get through to them when you call back. In this exceptional circumstance, consider diverting your calls to a mobile instead of using voicemail, the opposite of the usual solution.

Outcome By taking more control of your incoming calls you can reduce their impact on your time and minimize the resulting stress.

Variations This is very much a time management exercise. See Chapter 6 for further reading on time management.

Physical control	✪✪
Emotional/spiritual control	✪✪
Defence	✪✪✪✪
Fun	✪✪

5.67 Let the sunshine in

Preparation None.
Running time Five minutes.
Resources Sheet of paper; pen.
Frequency Once.

There is overwhelming evidence that a constant grey world without sunlight and warmth is depressing. This is backed up by everything from common sense to the suicide rate in countries with limited sunlight.

Given this is such a well-accepted fact, it's strange that we rarely take any notice of sunshine, except in recreation. Take a sheet of paper and draw a mind map or a simple list of ways you can get a little more sunshine into your life when you are under pressure. Examples might be: hold a meeting outside, take a five-minute break outside the building when it's sunny, use flexitime more spontaneously to react to good weather.

Stick up the sheet of paper somewhere that you can easily see it. Over the next couple of weeks, try to get some more sunshine into your working life.

Feedback This isn't a difficult exercise to put into practice, but it often isn't achieved. This is probably because we don't like the weather to take charge of our timetable, yet many of us have some flexibility over when we work. Why not make use of that sunshine? Remember the sunblock, though – the aim is to relieve stress, not to get burnt.

Outcome Getting a little sun in your life puts a spring in your step. You perform better, and you feel better. It's a natural stress tonic.

Variations If you are at the top of a large company, consider ways of changing the working environment to get more sunlight in. It is not a trivial problem, as you have to balance overheating and glare, but when done properly as at the award-winning British Airways headquarters building Waterside (where a glassed-over street links all the office buildings, providing a light, sunny environment in which all staff spend a fair amount of time), it really works. When you go to Waterside you can feel the stress slipping away.

Physical control	✪✪✪✪
Emotional/spiritual control	✪✪✪
Defence	✪✪
Fun	✪✪✪

5.68 Low power dressing

Preparation None.
Running time Five minutes.
Resources None.
Frequency Once.

The way we dress contributes to our state of relaxation and stress. Tight, formal clothes increase stress levels. Loose, informal clothes help us to relax. Be particularly wary about restrictions about the throat, chest and waist, which can all be significant contributors to stressing.

Spend a few minutes mapping out your week. Which clothes do you wear when? How do the different types of clothing make you feel? How can you get the positive feeling of power that formal dressing gives without adding to your stress levels with tight, stiff clothing? Look for opportunities to overthrow any dress code, at least part of the time.

Feedback When I worked in a corporate office daily I never questioned the need to wear a suit to work. Yet once you have managed to work for a while, still doing a high-pressure job but without the need to dress up for it, you can never go back. Yes you will wear a suit, but only where absolutely necessary. Look at what people wear when they come into work for a special effort at the weekend. If the clothes are suitable then, why aren't they at other times?

If you have to stay with tight clothing, accept the facts of life. It is natural as you grow older that your neck and waist will increase in size. You aren't fooling anyone by holding onto the 14-inch collars that fitted at college. All they do now is choke you through the day. If, under pressure, you feel the need to undo your collar button it's too tight. Either buy a new shirt or keep it undone.

Outcome Almost everyone who has moved to wearing more casual work clothes finds it a positive move. There are good physical reasons for avoiding tight, constricting clothes. Finding a way to wear casuals more often will help your underlying stress levels.

Variations None.

Physical control	✪✪✪✪
Emotional/spiritual control	✪✪✪
Defence	✪
Fun	✪✪✪

5.69 Go with the flow

Preparation None.
Running time 10 minutes.
Resources None.
Frequency Once.

This is only really for those who work in an organizational structure. Spend five minutes jotting down what organizational communications are routed through you. They might be formal, regular debriefings, like a cascade of management information, or might be simple chats with a group about how things are going.

Now look for the stress points in the communication structure. Should there be information flows in either direction that currently don't exist? Particularly look out for upward flows that are missing. Do staff have an opportunity to feed back responses to a downward communication, or to ask for extra information? Is there full disclosure of what is happening in the company?

Feedback Looking for problems in the flow of information is very valuable in determining where stress might be generated. We all thrive on communication. If we feel we don't know what is going on or, even worse, that things are being consciously held back from us, we will feel out of control and stress will grow.

Outcome Although the primary result of this exercise is to think of others, everything that applies to them also applies to you. Anything you can do to improve their communications will probably help you with yours, and hence with your stress.

Variations It's rather daring, but this technique is best used by also asking those involved what they feel is missing. Even if you can't deliver the answers yourself, it's worth asking and making sure that it is known just what is needed. As Ricardo Semler demonstrates in *Maverick!* (see Chapter 6 for details), even the least educated blue-collar workers can show an interest in company performance with appropriate help. Don't assume 'they' won't be interested.

Physical control	✪
Emotional/spiritual control	✪
Defence	✪✪✪✪
Fun	✪✪✪

5.70 Half full or half empty

Preparation None.
Running time One week.
Resources None.
Frequency Once.

Perception is amazingly important to stress. Our bodies are easily fooled at this gut level. You can generate unnecessary stress – or eradicate it – by modifying your state of mind.

Most of us are pessimistic part of the time; some make a career of it, always finding something to moan about.

Spend a few minutes thinking through the ways that you are naturally pessimistic and optimistic. Then, for the next week, be really conscious of how you are. Put in various places (beside your bed, in the car, on your desk) a little reminder of this exercise – a picture of a half-full glass. Whenever you get a chance to make an observation that could go either way, or even have a thought, force it into the optimistic. Don't look at a cloudy sky in the evening and say 'Looks like rain tomorrow', say 'It may well clear in the night.' Make the glass always half full.

Feedback There is a strong Pygmalion effect in action here. The more you force yourself to act optimistically, the more you will actually feel positive. The more you feel positive, the more you will feel in charge and the less stressed you will be. Usually, the difficulty is maintaining the stance – hence the little visual reminders. After a week you may well find it comes so naturally that you do it without being reminded.

Outcome Being optimistic comes naturally to most children, but (despite the fact most of us have pretty good lives) it gets worn away as we become adults. Give your natural optimism a revival course and help to release the stress.

Variations None.

Physical control	✪
Emotional/spiritual control	✪✪✪✪
Defence	✪✪✪✪
Fun	✪✪✪

6

MORE STRESS MANAGEMENT

FINDING OUT MORE

Stress management is a wide topic, covering self-help, health and business. This chapter gives some references for further reading, some suggestions for stress-relieving music and some online references to find out more about stress.

BOOKS

GENERAL

David Ashton (1993) *The 12-Week Executive Health Plan*, Kogan Page
Good health is one of the cornerstones of being able to manage stress. This readable book, which manages to avoid the tendency of the health movement to work with the fad-of-the-moment, is a good guide to getting something practical done about improving your health.

Cary L Cooper, Rachel Cooper and Lynn Eaker (1991) *Living with Stress*, Penguin
A good exploration of stress, what it is and where it comes from. Although not specifically business-oriented, spends quite a lot of time on workplace stress, including some slightly dated but nonetheless useful research. DIY stress questionnaires to assess your condition.

Lynn Fossum (1993) *Managing Anxiety*, Kogan Page
A quick guide to the nature of anxiety and how to conquer it. Fossum's book is short and has plenty of practical exercises to reduce this key component of stress.

Brenda O'Hanlon (1998) *Stress, The Commonsense Approach*, Newleaf
A good pocketbook giving a general overview of stress and how to deal with it. Gives rather a lot of space to alternative treatments and therapy, but otherwise well-balanced.

BUSINESS SPECIFIC

Peter E Makin and Patricia A Lindley (1991) *Positive Stress Management*, Kogan Page
Time management, good communication, relaxation and fitness come together to form the main parts of this practical guide to staying on top of work pressures. It also considers how we can stay in control and use others to manage stress.

Lesley Towner (1998) *Managing Employee Stress*, Kogan Page
One of the Better Management Skills series, aimed at giving a test-as-you-go run through stress in business. As the title suggests, concentrates solely on employees and takes something of an 'us and them' approach – but this does mean it gives useful information on legislation etc.

Stephen Williams (1994) *Managing Pressure For Peak Performance*, Kogan Page
The subtitle, 'The positive approach to stress' gives away the direction this interesting book takes. Rather than regarding stress as a necessary evil, it concentrates on achieving a balance, reducing stress where appropriate, but making use of stress where it is appropriate to achieve in the workplace.

TIME MANAGEMENT

Brian Clegg (1998) *The Chameleon Manager*, Butterworth Heinemann
This book takes the concept of time management into the wider sphere of gaining the skills needed to thrive in the workplace of the new millennium. It identifies management of creativity, communication and knowledge as the key requirements to working your way, and includes a different slant on time management from this perspective.

Brian Clegg (1999) *Instant Time Management*, Kogan Page
A companion volume in the Instant series, *Instant Time Management* provides a host of techniques for improving your time management without taking up too much time over it. Good time management enables you to deliver on your promises and ensure that your motivational programme is carried through – with poor time management, however good your intentions, you can fail to motivate.

Marion E Hayes (1996) *Make Every Minute Count*, Kogan Page
In the quick-fire Better Management Skills series, this is the only one of these books that is US written – but the subject varies little between countries. Even more checklists and questionnaires than Smith's book; this is an excellent way of getting started on the subject.

Ted Johns (1994) *Perfect Time Management*, Arrow
A handy pocketbook giving an overview of time management practice from a very pragmatic viewpoint. Varies between background and quite a lot of detail (eg suggested forms for the agenda of a meeting).

Lothar J Seiwert (1998) *Managing Your Time*, Kogan Page
A very visual book with lots of diagrams and plans and cartoons – it'll either impress you (as it has apparently more than 300,000 readers) or leave you cold. Particularly helpful if you like very specific guidance and information as juicy snippets.

Jane Smith (1997) *How to be a Better Time Manager*, Kogan Page
An Industrial Society sponsored volume, Smith's book takes an easy-to-read, no-nonsense approach to time management. A fair number of checklists and little questionnaires to fill in along the way, if you like that style.

TANGENTIAL

These books aren't about stress management *per se*, but provide valuable insights that will contribute greatly to an overall stress management programme.

Edward de Bono (1990) *Six Thinking Hats*, Penguin
Conflict and argument rarely lead to a constructive outcome and build up stress in all those involved. *Six Thinking Hats* is a mechanism for structuring meetings and discussions so that there is synergy rather than disagreement. This book covers the technique, probably de Bono's best known concept after lateral thinking, in great depth.

Ricardo Semler (1994) *Maverick!*, Arrow
This business biography is one of the best business books ever written. It describes how the author took a conservative engineering business in Brazil and turned it into a stunning example of how business should be undertaken. The relevance to stress management is how so many of the stress-inducing aspects of work, which we assume can't be changed, were thrown away. No policies and procedures manual. No specific working hours (and this includes what would have been production line workers before they got rid of the production line). No one who felt totally out of control in their job and thus stressed. It's remarkable.

MUSIC

There is a wide range of music that can prove relaxing and help with stress. You can buy specific stress reduction music and tapes, but it's best to sample a few different styles and see which suits you best. Here are a few areas to try out.

PRE-CLASSICAL CHURCH MUSIC

Some find the easy, chanting rhythms of plainsong particularly relaxing. There are usually CDs of plainsong in the popular classical sections of record stores. Alternatively try one of the modified plainsong CDs like *Visions* where early music is given a sympathetic 20th/21st century treatment.

If you like a little more depth to your music, but still want the spiritual content, there are many CDs of Tudor and Elizabethan church music, a period when the smooth intertwining of different musical lines was particularly prized, producing a vast range of stress-relieving options. Beginners should try a CD featuring the *Allegri Miserere*, one of the best known pieces of this style. Composers to look for include Byrd, Gibbons, Palestrina, Philips, Sheppard, Tallis, Taverner (not Tavener) and Tye.

CLASSICAL

As long as you remember that there is plenty of classical music that isn't suitable for stress relief (just think of Mars from the Planet Suite or the 1812 Overture), you should be fine. Look for calm, reflective pieces. A few pieces to look out for: Beethoven, *Pastoral Symphony*; Delius, *Summer Evening*; Elgar, *Enigma Variations*; Grieg, *Holberg Suite*; Pachelbel, *Canon*; Vaughan Williams, *The Lark Ascending*; Vivaldi, *Four Seasons*; Warlock, *Capriol Suite*.

FOLK ETC

In a recent test, John Denver's music was found to be amongst the most relaxing there was. Consider any of the 'soft' popular styles – as long as it isn't up-tempo and loud – or for that matter, the relaxed end of jazz. Folk is often a safe bet. You may find that you need to make a compilation from a number of CDs, as most will have a mix of low and high energy numbers.

MODERN 'SERIOUS' MUSIC

Much of the modern serious music that features on popular classical radio stations like Classic FM is repetitious and slow, like waves of sound passing across a beach. Try almost anything by Michael Nyman, for instance. You'll also find some TV-music, often available on CD, is surprisingly relaxing. Probably the best exponent is Barrington Pheloung, whose music for the TV series Morse typifies his relaxed exposition.

RELAXATION CDS

You can now find a wide range of CDs specifically designed to help you to relax. These are perfectly acceptable if you haven't the time to clarify your own tastes for music that will relieve stress, but if you have the chance, try some of the other categories, too.

ONLINE

Web site references soon date. Try putting 'stress management' or 'stress relief' into a search engine (such as **http://www.altavista.com**) or index (like **http://www.yahoo.com**), but be aware that you may need to filter some of the responses for rather liberal interpretations of stress relief. Here are a few sites current at the time of publishing:

- **http://www.capcenter.org/stress.html**
- **http://www.coolware.com/health/medical_reporter/stress.html**
- **http://www.isma.org.uk/**
- **http://www.mentalhealth.com/mag1/p51-str.html**
- **http://www.mindtools.com/smpage.html**
- **http://www.stresscure.com/**
- **http://www.stresstips.com/**

APPENDIX: THE SELECTOR

THE RANDOM SELECTOR

Take a watch with a second hand and note the number the second hand is pointing at now. Take that number technique from the list of 60 below.

No.	Ref.	Title
1	5.1	Little successes
2	5.2	Handling confrontation
3	5.3	Don't bury yourself
4	5.4	Capture ideas
5	5.5	Stress workout
6	5.6	Environmental stuff
7	5.9	You are what you eat
8	5.10	Breaks
9	5.13	Ritual relaxation
10	5.14	Mentor mine
11	5.16	Pushing waves
12	5.17	Breathing is good for you
13	5.18	Low-stress travel
14	5.19	It's good to talk
15	5.20	Pat on the back
16	5.21	Don't do that
17	5.22	Medicinal reading
18	5.23	Sulkers
19	5.24	Hitting target
20	5.25	Listen well
21	5.26	Commuter hell
22	5.27	Play!
23	5.28	Relaxing by numbers
24	5.29	I agree… ish
25	5.30	You can't take it with you
26	5.31	Café life
27	5.33	The spiritual path
28	5.34	Bureaucratic bounce-back
29	5.35	Because I'm worth it
30	5.36	E-mail it away
31	5.37	Walkies!
32	5.38	Sharing chores
33	5.39	Sleep!
34	5.40	I did that
35	5.43	Music soothes the savage breast
36	5.44	Fall-out shelters
37	5.46	Life, the universe and everything
38	5.47	Nemesis
39	5.48	Natural release
40	5.49	Information overload
41	5.50	Honesty
42	5.51	Different values
43	5.52	Stimulants stink
44	5.53	No news is good news
45	5.54	The timescales game
46	5.55	Setbacks
47	5.56	Boomerang compliments
48	5.58	Meditation
49	5.59	Pareto
50	5.60	Bully off
51	5.61	Pampering
52	5.62	Coping with change
53	5.63	Integral exercise
54	5.64	Going solo
55	5.65	Doing drugs
56	5.66	Phone control
57	5.67	Let the sunshine in
58	5.68	Low power dressing
59	5.69	Go with the flow
60	5.70	Half full or half empty

TECHNIQUES IN TIMING ORDER

This table sorts the techniques by the suggested timings. Those at the top take the longest, those towards the bottom are the quickest.

Ref.	Title
Week	
5.60	Bully off
5.70	Half full or half empty
Half day	
5.64	Going solo
30 minutes	
5.6	Environmental stuff
5.48	Natural release
5.63	Integral exercise
15 minutes	
5.5	Stress workout
5.9	You are what you eat
5.12	Touchy-smelly
5.14	Mentor mine
5.15	Stage fright
5.22	Medicinal reading
5.31	Café life
5.33	The spiritual path
5.37	Walkies!
5.61	Pampering
10 minutes	
5.2	Handling confrontation
5.3	Don't bury yourself
5.26	Commuter hell
5.27	Play!
5.30	You can't take it with you
5.34	Bureaucratic bounce-back
5.40	I did that
5.44	Fall-out shelters
5.46	Life, the universe and everything
5.47	Nemesis
5.49	Information overload
5.53	No news is good news
5.58	Meditation
5.62	Coping with change
5.65	Doing drugs
5.69	Go with the flow
Five minutes	
5.7	Laugh!
5.8	Unloading
5.10	Breaks
5.13	Ritual relaxation
5.16	Pushing waves
5.17	Breathing is good for you
5.18	Low-stress travel
5.19	It's good to talk
5.21	Don't do that
5.23	Sulkers
5.24	Hitting target
5.25	Listen well
5.28	Relaxing by numbers
5.29	I agree… ish
5.32	Get away
5.35	Because I'm worth it
5.38	Sharing chores
5.39	Sleep!
5.41	Broken record
5.42	Coherent discussion
5.43	Music soothes the savage breast
5.45	Pet solution
5.51	Different values
5.52	Stimulants stink
5.55	Setbacks
5.59	Pareto
5.66	Phone control
5.67	Let the sunshine in
5.68	Low power dressing
Two minutes	
5.1	Little successes
5.4	Capture ideas
5.11	Rage
5.20	Pat on the back
5.36	E-mail it away
5.50	Honesty
5.54	The timescales game
5.56	Boomerang compliments
5.57	Children

TECHNIQUES IN FREQUENCY ORDER

This table sorts the techniques by the frequency order. Those at the top are undertaken most frequently, those at the bottom once only.

Ref.	Title
Daily	
5.8	Unloading
5.22	Medicinal reading
Weekly	
5.26	Commuter hell
Regularly	
5.4	Capture ideas
5.17	Breathing is good for you
5.18	Low-stress travel
5.19	It's good to talk
5.20	Pat on the back
5.24	Hitting target
5.25	Listen well
5.27	Play!
5.36	E-mail it away
5.37	Walkies!
5.42	Coherent discussion
5.43	Music soothes the savage breast
5.45	Pet solution
5.48	Natural release
5.54	The timescales game
5.55	Setbacks
5.56	Boomerang compliments
5.57	Children
5.58	Meditation
5.63	Integral exercise
Occasionally	
5.11	Rage
5.12	Touchy-smelly
5.15	Stage fright
5.16	Pushing waves
5.28	Relaxing by numbers
5.29	I agree… ish
5.31	Café life
5.34	Bureaucratic bounce-back
5.38	Sharing chores
5.46	Life, the universe and everything
5.50	Honesty
5.61	Pampering
5.62	Coping with change
5.64	Going solo
Several times	
5.1	Little successes
5.21	Don't do that
Once	
5.2	Handling confrontation
5.3	Don't bury yourself
5.5	Stress workout
5.6	Environmental stuff
5.7	Laugh!
5.9	You are what you eat
5.10	Breaks
5.13	Ritual relaxation
5.14	Mentor mine
5.23	Sulkers
5.30	You can't take it with you
5.32	Get away
5.33	The spiritual path
5.35	Because I'm worth it
5.39	Sleep!
5.40	I did that
5.41	Broken record
5.44	Fall-out shelters
5.47	Nemesis
5.49	Information overload
5.51	Different values
5.52	Stimulants stink
5.53	No news is good news
5.59	Pareto
5.60	Bully off
5.65	Doing drugs
5.66	Phone control
5.67	Let the sunshine in
5.68	Low power dressing
5.69	Go with the flow
5.70	Half full or half empty

TECHNIQUES IN PHYSICAL CONTROL ORDER

This table sorts the techniques by the individual star ratings attached to each. Those at the top have the highest star rating, those at the bottom the lowest.

Ref.	Title
✪✪✪✪	
5.5	Stress workout
5.6	Environmental stuff
5.8	Unloading
5.9	You are what you eat
5.10	Breaks
5.12	Touchy-smelly
5.16	Pushing waves
5.17	Breathing is good for you
5.28	Relaxing by numbers
5.37	Walkies!
5.39	Sleep!
5.48	Natural release
5.52	Stimulants stink
5.63	Integral exercise
5.65	Doing drugs
5.67	Let the sunshine in
5.68	Low power dressing
✪✪✪	
5.7	Laugh!
5.18	Low-stress travel
5.21	Don't do that
5.45	Pet solution
5.56	Boomerang compliments
5.58	Meditation
5.59	Pareto
5.61	Pampering
✪✪	
5.11	Rage
5.13	Ritual relaxation
5.15	Stage fright
5.19	It's good to talk
5.20	Pat on the back
5.26	Commuter hell
5.27	Play!
5.30	You can't take it with you
5.31	Café life
5.32	Get away
5.38	Sharing chores
5.44	Fall-out shelters
5.47	Nemesis
5.57	Children
5.62	Coping with change
5.64	Going solo
5.66	Phone control
✪	
5.1	Little successes
5.2	Handling confrontation
5.3	Don't bury yourself
5.4	Capture ideas
5.14	Mentor mine
5.22	Medicinal reading
5.23	Sulkers
5.24	Hitting target
5.25	Listen well
5.29	I agree… ish
5.33	The spiritual path
5.34	Bureaucratic bounce-back
5.35	Because I'm worth it
5.36	E-mail it away
5.40	I did that
5.41	Broken record
5.42	Coherent discussion
5.43	Music soothes the savage breast
5.46	Life, the universe and everything
5.49	Information overload
5.50	Honesty
5.51	Different values
5.53	No news is good news
5.54	The timescales game
5.55	Setbacks
5.60	Bully off
5.69	Go with the flow
5.70	Half full or half empty

TECHNIQUES IN EMOTIONAL/SPIRITUAL CONTROL ORDER

This table sorts the techniques by the team star ratings attached to each. Those at the top have the highest star rating, those at the bottom the lowest.

Ref.	Title
✪✪✪✪	
5.1	Little successes
5.7	Laugh!
5.11	Rage
5.13	Ritual relaxation
5.14	Mentor mine
5.19	It's good to talk
5.20	Pat on the back
5.22	Medicinal reading
5.31	Café life
5.32	Get away
5.33	The spiritual path
5.35	Because I'm worth it
5.40	I did that
5.43	Music soothes the savage breast
5.44	Fall-out shelters
5.46	Life, the universe and everything
5.51	Different values
5.57	Children
5.58	Meditation
5.61	Pampering
5.62	Coping with change
5.70	Half full or half empty
✪✪✪	
5.2	Handling confrontation
5.3	Don't bury yourself
5.4	Capture ideas
5.10	Breaks
5.12	Touchy-smelly
5.15	Stage fright
5.16	Pushing waves
5.18	Low-stress travel
5.21	Don't do that
5.24	Hitting target
5.25	Listen well
5.26	Commuter hell
5.27	Play!
5.28	Relaxing by numbers
5.30	You can't take it with you
5.37	Walkies!
5.38	Sharing chores
5.39	Sleep!
5.42	Coherent discussion
5.45	Pet solution
5.47	Nemesis
5.48	Natural release
5.53	No news is good news
5.54	The timescales game
5.55	Setbacks
5.56	Boomerang compliments
5.64	Going solo
5.67	Let the sunshine in
5.68	Low power dressing
✪✪	
5.5	Stress workout
5.6	Environmental stuff
5.8	Unloading
5.9	You are what you eat
5.17	Breathing is good for you
5.23	Sulkers
5.29	I agree… ish
5.34	Bureaucratic bounce-back
5.36	E-mail it away
5.41	Broken record
5.49	Information overload
5.50	Honesty
5.52	Stimulants stink
5.60	Bully off
5.63	Integral exercise
5.66	Phone control
✪	
5.59	Pareto
5.65	Doing drugs
5.69	Go with the flow

TECHNIQUES IN DEFENCE ORDER

This table sorts the techniques by the group star ratings attached to each. Those at the top have the highest star rating, those at the bottom the lowest.

Ref.	Title
✪✪✪✪	
5.2	Handling confrontation
5.3	Don't bury yourself
5.4	Capture ideas
5.11	Rage
5.23	Sulkers
5.24	Hitting target
5.25	Listen well
5.27	Play!
5.30	You can't take it with you
5.32	Get away
5.34	Bureaucratic bounce-back
5.36	E-mail it away
5.41	Broken record
5.42	Coherent discussion
5.46	Life, the universe and everything
5.47	Nemesis
5.49	Information overload
5.53	No news is good news
5.54	The timescales game
5.55	Setbacks
5.56	Boomerang compliments
5.60	Bully off
5.66	Phone control
5.69	Go with the flow
5.70	Half full or half empty
✪✪✪	
5.10	Breaks
5.15	Stage fright
5.18	Low-stress travel
5.26	Commuter hell
5.29	I agree… ish
5.31	Café life
5.33	The spiritual path
5.35	Because I'm worth it
5.37	Walkies!
5.38	Sharing chores

Ref.	Title
5.44	Fall-out shelters
5.50	Honesty
5.57	Children
5.59	Pareto
✪✪	
5.5	Stress workout
5.6	Environmental stuff
5.7	Laugh!
5.13	Ritual relaxation
5.14	Mentor mine
5.19	It's good to talk
5.20	Pat on the back
5.22	Medicinal reading
5.28	Relaxing by numbers
5.39	Sleep!
5.51	Different values
5.61	Pampering
5.62	Coping with change
5.63	Integral exercise
5.67	Let the sunshine in
✪	
5.1	Little successes
5.8	Unloading
5.9	You are what you eat
5.12	Touchy-smelly
5.16	Pushing waves
5.17	Breathing is good for you
5.21	Don't do that
5.40	I did that
5.43	Music soothes the savage breast
5.45	Pet solution
5.48	Natural release
5.52	Stimulants stink
5.58	Meditation
5.64	Going solo
5.65	Doing drugs
5.68	Low power dressing

TECHNIQUES IN FUN ORDER

This table sorts the techniques by the fun star ratings attached to each. Those at the top have the highest star rating, those at the bottom the lowest.

Ref.	Title
✪✪✪✪	
5.7	Laugh!
5.20	Pat on the back
5.22	Medicinal reading
5.27	Play!
5.31	Café life
5.32	Get away
5.43	Music soothes the savage breast
5.45	Pet solution
5.61	Pampering
✪✪✪	
5.1	Little successes
5.6	Environmental stuff
5.12	Touchy-smelly
5.13	Ritual relaxation
5.14	Mentor mine
5.16	Pushing waves
5.19	It's good to talk
5.26	Commuter hell
5.28	Relaxing by numbers
5.34	Bureaucratic bounce-back
5.35	Because I'm worth it
5.37	Walkies!
5.40	I did that
5.44	Fall-out shelters
5.48	Natural release
5.49	Information overload
5.53	No news is good news
5.56	Boomerang compliments
5.58	Meditation
5.63	Integral exercise
5.64	Going solo
5.67	Let the sunshine in
5.68	Low power dressing
5.69	Go with the flow
5.70	Half full or half empty
✪✪	
5.2	Handling confrontation

Ref.	Title
5.3	Don't bury yourself
5.4	Capture ideas
5.5	Stress workout
5.8	Unloading
5.9	You are what you eat
5.10	Breaks
5.11	Rage
5.15	Stage fright
5.17	Breathing is good for you
5.18	Low-stress travel
5.21	Don't do that
5.23	Sulkers
5.24	Hitting target
5.25	Listen well
5.29	I agree… ish
5.30	You can't take it with you
5.33	The spiritual path
5.36	E-mail it away
5.38	Sharing chores
5.39	Sleep!
5.41	Broken record
5.42	Coherent discussion
5.46	Life, the universe and everything
5.50	Honesty
5.51	Different values
5.52	Stimulants stink
5.54	The timescales game
5.55	Setbacks
5.57	Children
5.59	Pareto
5.62	Coping with change
5.66	Phone control
✪	
5.47	Nemesis
5.60	Bully off
5.65	Doing drugs